SOPHOCLES ANTIGONE & OEDIPUS THE KING

A Companion to the Penguin Translation
of Robert Fagles
with Introduction and Commentary by

John Wilkins
Lecturer in Classics, University of Aberdeen, and

Matthew Macleod
Formerly Lecturer in Classics, University of
Southampton

D0145696

Published by Bristol Classical Press
General Editor: John H. Betts

First published in 1987 by
Bristol Classical Press
an imprint of
Gerald Duckworth & Co. Ltd
The Old Piano Factory
48 Hoxton Square, London N1 6PB

Reprinted 1990, 1992, 1994

Companion to *Antigone* © 1987 by John Wilkins
Companion to *Oedipus the King* © 1987 by Matthew Macleod

A catalogue record for this book is available
from the British Library

ISBN 0-86292-240-2

Printed in Great Britain by
Booksprint, Bristol

Contents

Preface   4
General Introduction   5
Select Bibliography   14
Antigone
    Introduction to *Antigone*   19
    Companion to *Antigone*   27
    Appendix   69
    Select Index and Glossary   71
Oedipus the King
    Introduction to *Oedipus the King*   75
    Companion to *Oedipus the King*   80

Preface

This Companion is for use alongside the 1984 Penguin translation of Sophocles *The Three Theban Plays* by Robert Fagles, with introduction and brief notes by Bernard Knox. In order to minimise duplication of material 'see Knox' is used throughout to refer to the Penguin editorial material.

O.T. is used as the abbreviation for *Oedipus the King* (i.e. its alternative title *Oedipus Tyrannus*), and *O.C.* for *Oedipus at Colonus*. The line numbers of *O.T.*, *O.C.* and *Antigone* referred to are to the Penguin edition; other references to ancient sources are to the original line number or location except for references to Aeschylus *Agamemnon*, *Libation Bearers* and *Eumenides*, which are to the Penguin translation of Robert Fagles (1977).

John Wilkins is responsible for the Companion to the *Antigone*, Matthew Macleod for the Companion to *Oedipus the King* and for the General Introduction.

General Introduction

1. THE DEVELOPMENT OF TRAGEDY AT ATHENS

In the field of drama as in many other branches of Greek culture Athens played the leading role. The three great tragic poets, Aeschylus, Sophocles and Euripides were all Athenian, as were the comic poets Aristophanes and Menander. Their tragedies and comedies were usually performed at the theatre of Dionysus at festivals in his honour, the Dionysia. Dionysus was not only the god of wine but also of vegetation and fertility. In this capacity he was associated with the release of mass emotion, of powerful sensual and irrational impulses (see Euripides' *Bacchae*). The controlled ritual of the Dionysia was considered a necessary purge of such impulses; see Aristotle's analysis of the effect of tragedy in *Poetics*.

Although Athens can claim the credit for perfecting tragedy and comedy, the germs of both probably came from the Dorians, Greeks who spoke a different dialect from the Athenians and lived mainly to the south in the Peloponnese. Tragedy probably developed from Dorian choral performances. Note that a chorus is not simply a band of singers or a song by such a band, as it means today. The original meaning of the word *choros* was 'dance', but it soon came to be applied to a performance where the dance was accompanied by song, or to the group of performers who gave such an act.

The vital step towards tragedy was taken at Athens by Thespis, who added an actor to his chorus of dancers and singers and so made the performance dramatic. The Greek work for actor was *hypocritēs*, from which one gets English 'hypocrite', really meaning 'one who puts on an act'. The original meaning of the word, however, was probably 'answerer', someone who answers the chorus, though an alternative derivation is someone who interprets a role. Thespis seems first to have produced a tragedy at a festival of Dionysus in about 534 B.C. during the rule of the tyrant Pisistratus who was a great patron of the arts.

The inscription which records Thespis' performance at Athens mentions a goat as the prize and this may explain the name tragedy, which literally means 'goat-song' in Greek. If so, it was a song performed in competition for a goat as prize; alternatively the name may mean performance at a festival where a goat was sacrificed. At any rate it seems probable that a goat met its doom at the goat-song to the delight of Dionysus, as the destructive goat would be a natural enemy of the god of vegetation and the vine. A less popular theory is that tragedy got its name because the tragic chorus were originally men dressed up as goats, but there is little evidence that this was the case.

Thespis, then, added one actor to give answers to the chorus. The second actor was introduced by Aeschylus. Aeschylus' first tragedy probably fell within the Olympiad, or period of four years, 499-6 B.C., although his earliest extant datable play was the *Persians* of 472 B.C. The third actor was, according to Aristotle, added by Sophocles, although other sources ascribe this innovation to Aeschylus. At any rate the third actor was used by Aeschylus in his later plays including the Oresteia (*Agamemnon, Choephoroi* and *Eumenides*) of 458 B.C. With the introduction of the third actor, tragedy had reached what Aristotle calls it *physis*, its natural state, and thereafter till the end of the century and the latest plays, *O.C.* and Euripides' *Bacchae* and *Iphigenia in Aulis*, the overall form of tragedies remained much the same.

2. THE LIFE AND TIMES OF SOPHOCLES
The lifetime of Sophocles spanned the greatest years of Athens. He was born at Colonus, the setting for *O.C.*, in about 496 B.C., around the time when Aeschylus was producing his first plays. He would have been old enough to appreciate the victories achieved by the Greeks and the Athenians in particular in the Persian Wars of 480-79, soon to be dramatised by Aeschylus in the *Persae*, the only surviving tragedy on a historical as opposed to a mythological theme. He was victorious in his first tragic competition in 468, even defeating Aeschylus, but did not compete in 467 when Aeschylus won with his *Theban trilogy*. Whether he competed against Aeschylus' victorious *Oresteia* in 458 or not, we do not know. The year 456 marked the death of Aeschylus and the next year saw Euripides come third in his first competition.

Athens was now at the height of her power as head of the Delian League and her leading politician Pericles transferred the Treasury of the League from the island of Delos to Athens. In 443 Sophocles was appointed to one year's office as *hellēnotamias*, one of the important magistrates in charge of the funds of the League, and in 441 was elected to be one of the ten *stratēgoi* or 'generals' along with Pericles, and was involved in suppressing a revolt against Athens and the League by the islanders of Samos. The Peloponnesian War started in 431, followed in the next year by the outbreak of plague at Athens. After the crisis caused by the disaster in Sicily in 413 Athens was for a time governed by ten *probouloi*, counsellors extraordinary, one of whom was a Sophocles, presumably our poet. Like Euripides, he did not survive to see Athens' final defeat at Aegispotami in 405 and her surrender in 404, dying in 406; their deaths are referred to by Aristophanes in his play, the *Frogs* (405). Many of the anecdotes about him which are related in a Life attached to some of the medieval manuscripts are mistrusted, but we can at least be sure that he was outstandingly musical and pious.

He is credited with 123 plays, and with either 24 or 20 victories (accounts vary; this would mean 96, or 80, of his plays were successful, if each victory involved three tragedies plus a satyric drama; see below); the tradition also states that he never came third. If this is true and *O.T.* was defeated by Aeschylus' nephew Philocles, as we learn from a writer of the second century A.D., it follows that *O.T.* and the plays with it came second. Many fragments of his plays have survived, including much of a satyric drama, *Ichneutai* (*The Trackers*), on the birth of Hermes. Only two of the seven complete plays can be dated with certainty; *Philoctetes* won first prize in 409 and *O.C.* was only produced posthumously in 401. (Cicero and Plutarch record the tradition that Sophocles in extreme old age was sued by his sons for the control of his property on the grounds of senile debility but got off by reading from *O.C.*). *Ajax* and *Ant.* seem to be the earliest plays, with *Ant.* to be dated about 442 if we can believe the story that Sophocles was appointed *stratēgos* on the strength of it. Style and content suggest that *Trachiniae*, *O.T.* and *Electra* came between *Ant.* and *Philoctetes*. Although *O.T.* cannot be given a precise date, the references to the plague *may* suggest a date within a few years after 430. If this is so, it would be of much the same date as Euripides' *Hippolytus* which won in 428.

3. THE DIONYSIA

Unlike a modern play a tragedy or comedy was a one-off competitive performance in an open-air theatre on a public holiday which was also a religious festival in honour of Dionysus. There were three separate festivals of Dionysus involving drama; the Rural Dionysia in December and the Lenaea in January were purely local Athenian affairs; but the major festival, the City or Great Dionysia, held in late March or early April when the seas were navigable again, was open to foreigners, including visiting ambassadors and representatives of Athens' allies bringing tribute for the Treasury of the Delian League, and, like the Parthenon and Propylaea on the Acropolis above, was a source of patriotic pride to the Athenians.

On the first day of the city Dionysia the statue of Dionysus would be escorted through the streets in a ceremonial procession which would include the *choregoi*, rich Athenians who paid for the expenses of a chorus out of their own pockets. In the evening would follow a *kōmos* or procession of drunken revellers; the name *cōmos* will be familiar from Milton's Masque, but it also is the derivation of 'comedy' which is the song of the *kōmos* (the alternative derivation from *kōmē*, village, is generally rejected). Then would follow four days of drama, though this was cut to three as a wartime economy measure. In peacetime there would have been one day with one comedy by each of five poets, followed by three days each devoted to four plays by one tragic poet. In wartime, however, it seems there were only three days of drama, each with four plays by one tragic poet followed by one comedy.

The four plays of the tragic poet usually consisted of three tragedies followed by a slightly less formal play called a satyric drama, because its chorus were Satyrs, mythical creatures half horse, half man, as often seen in vase paintings. Aeschylus' sets of three tragedies usually covered successive stages in the same family myth and were called trilogies, whereas Sophocles and Euripides preferred unconnected plays. The poet's first step would be to get the senior archon of the year to 'give him a chorus' and presumably also a *choregus*, but at least after 449, when acting prizes for protagonists started (protagonists were actors taking the leading part), those previously selected would be assigned to the three poets by lot. The state would pay the poet, the actors and the cost of their costumes, but all choral expenses would be met by the *choregus*. The poet would normally be his own producer, though he could get help with the training of the chorus. Shortly before the festival the poet and his actors would appear in public at a ceremony called the *prōagōn* to announce the subject of his plays.

The audience had to pay for admission, though Pericles inaugurated a fund to enable poorer citizens to attend. Women could probably attend tragedies only, and perhaps had to sit separately. Attendance by slaves would be exceptional. The best seats would be reserved for priests, particularly the priest of Dionysus, officials, public benefactors and orphans whose fathers had died in battle. We do not know how many the original theatre held, though the capacity of the late fourth century (Lycurgan) theatre we see today is estimated at between thirteen and seventeen thousand. The original seating arrangements were primitive and in view of the long day ahead of them (tragedies started early in the morning) the audience might well bring cushions, food and drink. Audiences were noisy in applause and disapproval, sometimes even pelting actors with fruit and confectionery.

The Rural Dionysia was celebrated at various dates in December by the demes or districts of Attica. The central feature of the festival was a procession escorting a huge replica of a phallus, the male genital organ, but some demes also held dramatic and/or dithyrambic contests, those at the Peiraeus, the port of Athens, being the most important. The Lenaea in January was perhaps so called from *Lēnai*, a name for Bacchae or Maenads, female devotees of Dionysus. The celebrations may have involved an all-night revel by women; they included a procession and dramatic contests for poets and actors with two tragedies by each of two poets and one comedy by each of five poets, reduced to three during the Peloponnesian War.

4. THE STRUCTURE OF TRAGEDIES

The cast consisted of a chorus of fifteen, three actors and, if needed, extras who would appear without speaking. The actors were all men and wore masks and so were able to take several roles or even to share roles between them. (Thus in the *O.T.* there are eight dramatis personae, but only a maximum of three of them is allowed to take part in the dialogue at any one time. Extras for non-speaking parts, *kōpha prosōpa*, would be needed for the suppliants in the opening scene, for various servants, and for Antigone and Ismene at the end).

Tragedies have a formalised and distinctive structure not immediately obvious to readers of translations, being divided mainly into dialogue

9

scenes and choral odes. The traditional names for the various subdivisions of tragedy are taken from Chapter 12 of the *Poetics*, the opening dialogue scene being called the 'prologue', subsequent dialogue scenes 'episodes' and the final scene the *exodos*; between the dialogue scenes come choral odes of which the first is called the *parodos* and later ones *stasima*. Thus the component parts of the *O.T.* are:

prologue	1-168 (lines numbered as in Fagles' Penguin)
parodos	168-244
1st episode	245-526
1st stasimon	526-572
2nd episode	573-953
2nd stasimon	954-997
3rd episode	998-1194
3rd stasimon	1195-1214
4th episode	1215-1310
4th stasimon	1311-1350
Exodos	1351-1684

The dialogue scenes (prologue, episodes and exodos) are formally declaimed in iambics, the metre which Aristotle calls the natural rhythm of human speech. The diction is dignified in keeping with the exalted station of the heroes and princes who are the chief characters. The tragic poets also tended to confine their vocabulary to a limited range of words which had the sanction of precedent.

The prologue is followed by the first choral song, usually called the *parodos*, or passage-song, because in early plays it was a marching song as the chorus processed along the side-passages or parodoi into the orchestra. Once in the orchestra, they normally remain there throughout the play, as indeed they do in the *O.T.* The chorus wear masks and are accompanied by an unmasked piper, *aulētēs*, playing the *aulos* or double pipe, as seen on many vase-paintings, e.g. the Pronomos Vase. (Choral odes are often called lyrics, which is misleading as the accompanying instrument was not normally the lyre or harp.) The member of a tragic chorus had to work far harder than a chorister in a modern opera, as he had not only to sing but also to dance, adding appropriate gestures. The dance was no doubt an energetic performance, if one may judge from the vigour and zest with which Greek men today perform the *Kalamatianos*.

Choral odes were very complicated in their construction, consisting of pairs of stanzas with each second stanza corresponding exactly in every detail with the preceding one. Sophoclean choral odes usually have two or three such pairs of stanzas, each consisting of, on average, about ten lines of varying lengths and rhythms; for example the first two stanzas of the first ode of the *O.T.* (168ff.), each have 96 syllables, with exact metrical correspondence and presumably also exact correspondence of the music and dance steps. The first stanza of each pair was called a *strophē* (turn), perhaps because the chorus turned and danced in one direction, and the corresponding stanza was the *antistrophē* (counter-turn), during which they returned to their original position using exactly the same dancing steps and exactly the same tune. The metres, music and dancing would be appropriate to the emotions of the chorus at that point in the play, e.g. expressing joy at *O.T.* 1195 and misery at 1311. Choruses therefore needed careful training and this was the poet's personal responsibility.

The musical element in tragedy was not confined to the choral odes; accompaniment was provided by the piper at other points which varied from play to play, with the details variously interpreted by scholars. For a full discussion see A. Pickard-Cambridge. It seems, however, that actors would be called on to use recitative (speech to the accompaniment of the *aulos*) or even occasionally to sing: Euripides was criticised for the excessive use of monodies (solos) by his actors. The *kommos*, a musical interlude shared by chorus and actors, was a regular feature of tragedies, being a combination of lyrics and iambics with the voices of the chorus and of one or more actors alternating and, like the choral odes, divided into corresponding strophes and antistrophes.

Modern producers of ancient tragedies can therefore hardly hope exactly to reproduce every detail of the original plays, but the overall effect ot a modern audience would be something like seeing elements of Shakespeare, Verdi and Tschaïkovsky combined within each of four plays performed in succession in the open air on Good Friday or Easter Sunday.

5. THE PHYSICAL APPEARANCE OF THE THEATRE

A precise description of the Theatre of Dionysus as it existed in Athens when *O.T.* was produced is impossible as the evidence from literature, art and archaeology is uncertain and incomplete. Photographs of the theatre at Epidaurus and of the remains of the theatre at Athens are useful for giving a general impression. It should be noted, however, that the Epidaurus theatre was later, larger and more elaborate and that the theatre remains visible in Athens today are also of a later, larger and more permanent theatre. (Fuller discussion of the ancient theatre will be found in Erika Simon pp.1-33, H.C. Baldry pp.36-53 and the *Cambridge History of Classical Literature* Vol. 1 pp.263-81.)

The Greek word *theatron* means 'place for watching' and Greek theatres, including that of Dionysus at Athens, were located where nature provided amenities for spectators and good acoustics, often in a roughly semi-circular hollow in a hillside. The central feature of the theatre was the orchestra ('dancing-place') which was occupied by the chorus. It was usually circular and perhaps originated from the circular threshing floors used not only for threshing grain but also for drying grapes; note here the connection with Dionysus, the god of the vine. Many circular threshing floors hollowed out of hillsides can still be seen in Greece today and are still used for communal dancing. Although the Sophoclean chorus probably only had fifteen members, called *choreutai*, the orchestra was large enough to accommodate the larger chorus of fifty used for the dithyrambs, hymns in honour of Dionysus, which were also performed at the theatre in Athens.

Behind the orchestra was the proscenium, a long narrow acting area, perhaps on a wooden platform slightly above the level of the orchestra and connected to it by one or two steps. Behind the proscenium was the *skēnē*. (*Skēnē* usually means 'tent' or 'hut', so indicating that its original purpose was that of actors' dressing-room and shelter, the ancient equivalent of the 'green room'.) The *skēnē* was a long, wooden stage building, painted in perspective and often, as in *O.T.*, representing the front of a palace. It contained at least one actual door, through which characters could come and go. Another means of entrances and exits was provided by the long side-passages (*parodoi*) in front of the proscenium and on each side of the orchestra. These passages were also used by the chorus in making their entry (hence the *parodos*) and by the audience before and after the performance.

Other features of the theatre, though not used in *O.T.* were the crane and the *ekkyklēma*. The crane (*mēchanē* = 'machine') suspended gods in mid-air. It would have been used by Sophocles at the start of the *Ajax* and end of the *Philoctetes*, but was specially common at the end of Euripides' plays. The *ekkyklēma* was a large wheeled trolley which could be pushed out through the doors of a palace to reveal to the audience a tableau of the scene, often of carnage, within, e.g. Clytemnestra standing over the bodies of Agamemnon and Cassandra in the *Agamemnon*, or Orestes and Pylades with the corpse of Clytemnestra in Sophocles' *Electra*.

Select Bibliography

Greek Tragedy

Brown A.L. *A New Companion to Greek Tragedy* (Beckenham 1983)
Taplin O. *Greek Tragedy in Action* (London 1978)
Vickers B. *Towards Greek Tragedy* (London 1973)

The Theatre

Buxton R.G. *Sophocles* (Greece & Rome New Surveys in the Classics no. 16) (Oxford 1984)
Gould J. in *Cambridge History of Classical Literature* Vol 1 pp.263-81
Parke H.W. *Festivals of the Athenians* (London 1977)
Pickard-Cambridge A. *The Dramatic Festivals of Athens* (2nd edn. Oxford 1968)
Simon E. *The Ancient Theatre* (London 1982)

Sophocles

Burton R.W.B. *The Chorus in Sophocles' Tragedies* (Oxford 1980)
Easterling P.E. in *Cambridge History of Classical Literature* Vol 1 pp.295-316
Gellie G.H. *Sophocles : A Reading* (Melbourne 1972)
Knox B.M.W. *The Heroic Temper : Studies in Sophoclean Tragedy* (Berkeley and Los Angeles 1964)
Lesky A. *Greek Tragedy* (London 1978) ch. 5
Reinhardt K. *Sophokles* (Engl. edn. Oxford 1979)
Segal C. *Tragedy and Civilisation : An Interpretation of Sophocles* (Cambridge Mass. 1981)
Sutton D.F. *The Lost Sophocles* (Lanham 1984)
Whitman C.H. *Sophocles : A Study of Heroic Humanism* (Cambridge Mass. 1951)
Winnington-Ingram R.P. *Sophocles : An Interpretation* (Cambridge 1980)

Antigone

Goheen R.F. *The Imagery of Sophocles' Antigone* (Princeton 1951)
Segal C. 'Sophocles' Praise of Man and the Conflicts of the *Antigone'*
in Woodard T.M. *Sophocles : A Collection of Critical Essays*
(Englewood Cliffs N.J. 1966)

Oedipus the King

Dodds E.R. 'On Misunderstanding the Oedipus Rex' *Greece and Rome* (1966) pp.37-49
Knox B.M.W. *Word and Action* (Baltimore 1979) pp.87-111

Antigone

Introduction to Antigone

1. THE BACKGROUND

Antigone was written and performed shortly before 440 BC in one of the most exciting decades for Athens in the fifth century. In Athens the democracy was expressing its self-confidence in the great building programme which included the Parthenon (begun in 447); in the allied states Athens was flexing her muscles as an imperial power, especially against Samos in the last years of the decade; in the arts, philosophers and historians, painters and sculptors (Pheidias' statue of Athene in the Parthenon was completed in 438) converged on Athens, and drama flourished in the comedies and tragedies performed at the city festivals. At the heart of all this was Pericles, fighting off his political enemies, glorifying Athens with temples, encouraging strong empire, and surrounded with a circle of artists and intellectuals, including Pheidias and the philosopher Anaxagoras.

The drama at the city festivals was inevitably influenced by the city's fortunes. Comedy pilloried Pericles and his circle as its most obvious target, and tragedy also reflected Periclean Athens, though in less easily defined ways. Sophocles in his two surviving plays of the Periclean period, *Antigone* and *Oedipus the King* has characters, Creon and Oedipus, who at times speak in a way reminiscent of Pericles' own words. Pericles is in a subtle way projected on to a character, presumably with no direct intention of praise or blame; but the question arises, what is Sophocles saying about his contemporary world? Particularly when characters and chorus sometimes also speak and sing in ways borrowed from the latest writers and thinkers of the day.

Ancient sources that are reasonably reliable report that *Antigone* was so great a success that the Athenians elected Sophocles into high office (as *stratēgos*) and that he took part in some of the Samos campaigns as a junior colleague of Pericles. The play has found many admirers ever since (see below).

2. THE MYTH

On the one hand is the contemporary flavour, on the other the basic structure of the play, which is built around a stark incident in the mythical past, the burial by Antigone of her brother Polynices when forbidden to do so by King Creon. The story is part of the ancient myth of the house of Laius and Oedipus, Kings of Thebes. Oedipus killed his father Laius without realising who he was, married his mother Jocasta, had four incestuous children, two sons Eteocles and Polynices, and two daughters Ismene and Antigone; only then did he discover his crimes. He blinded himself and Jocasta killed herself. Creon, Jocasta's brother, ruled Thebes for a time, and was replaced by Eteocles. But Polynices soon argued that the throne was his and brought six warriors and an army from the Peloponnese to win back the throne. The seven attacking heroes were matched by seven Thebans, and among the casualties Eteocles and Polynices died at each other's hand. Creon returned to power, and issued an edict that honourable burial was to be accorded the patriot Eteocles, and no burial at all to the traitor Polynices. At this point *Antigone* begins. For further details see Knox, Penguin introduction pp.27ff.

The dispute over the burial was in Sophocles' time a little-quoted aftermath of the Seven against Thebes story, but for Sophocles it has two important aspects, burial and an act of defiance by a woman. The ritual of burial figures largely in the seven Sophocles plays to survive: in *Ajax* burial is refused to a would-be assassin, in *Antigone* to Polynices the traitor. In *Oedipus at Colonus* there is argument over where Oedipus should be buried. For Sophocles, burial is a religious necessity, but when complicated by crime and guilt, that burial can lay bare deep religious and cultural beliefs. Antigone's femininity has a similar importance; women have a private rather than public life in fifth century Athens; this life is often offset in tragedy by the dominant presence of women in myth, often as a dangerous force. In *Antigone* Antigone acts fearlessly and publically, and is ultimately shown to be right in her stand, but her attitude and views are constantly criticised by Creon and the chorus, who find her behaviour abnormal and worrying. This tension is again fruitful for the thought of the play.

The house of Oedipus serves as a sinister background to these themes. Characters and chorus refer back to the crimes of Oedipus, and leave the audience feeling uneasy over Antigone's defence of family and kin: past crimes seem in part to undermine her case. This stress on the past in *Antigone* is to be contrasted with *Oedipus the King* where Sophocles at all times strives to eliminate ancestral crimes from the play in order to focus all responsibility on to Oedipus and his actions. This comparison shows among other things how Sophocles shapes the same story to very different effect to suit his dramatic design.

3. THE CHARACTERS

Antigone is forceful, self-sufficient, uncompromising and extreme; for her, actions must be bold and visible and public. The unorthodoxy of such conduct in a woman is highlighted by Ismene who submits to the male ruler and head of the household as a Greek woman conventionally did. Where Ismene remains indoors, Antigone moves outside in the man's world (see 111-16, 469ff.). Antigone seizes the initiative and buries her brother in a token burial, without waiting for the male authorities to play their part. The contrast with Ismene is a device Sophocles uses elsewhere: in *Electra* a 'normal' character, Chrysothemis, throws into relief the extreme nature of the main character, her sister Electra.

Creon shares some characteristics with Antigone; a stubborn refusal to change, an insistence that he is right, and lack of interest in any other point of view. There are strong passions in his nature which lead to anger and conduct verging on the tyrannical. It must be said, though, that much of Creon's vigorous argument may have been sympathetically received by the audience. His case for the supremacy of the state is echoed in the Funeral Speech of Pericles (Thucydides 2.35-46) where the benefits of power are set beside the less pleasant aspects. And the refusal to bury a traitor seems to reflect Athenian practice.

There has been much argument over who is the main character, Antigone the unflinching defender of her beliefs, or Creon the tragic figure who must suffer and learn from his errors. The argument is unimportant, but it should be noted that Antigone conforms to a pattern of character found elsewhere in Sophoclean heroes/heroines, in Oedipus, Philoctetes and particularly Ajax. They insist stubbornly and unflinchingly on the line they have adopted; they are lonely and isolated from the lesser characters; they have an alarming fierceness. The best analysis of this type of character can be found in B.M.W. Knox *The Heroic Temper*.

The lesser characters, Ismene, Haemon the hot-headed lover trying to reconcile the clash between his father and fiancee, the sentry and Eurydice (Creon's wife) have personal characteristics, but, more importantly, contribute to the meaning of the play. Scholars debate the extent to which these and all characters in Greek tragedy are made either psychologically convincing individuals or vehicles for the poet's rhetoric and thought, or both. The most accessible account is by P.E. Easterling in *Greece and Rome* 25 (1977) 121-9, but she in my view goes too far in detecting psychological detail. The characters are given sufficient colour to make them credible human beings, and no more. Where some in the audience may for example put Antigone's apparent change of mind down to her 'character', I would prefer to account for it in terms of the themes of the play: see note on 900ff. And does Antigone love Haemon? The question is important, for at 900ff. Antigone suddenly begins to speak of marriage after earlier speaking lovingly only of the dead. Is this a matter of ' character'? Sophocles seems to give us no help in answering positively; see notes on 86 and on 905-8.

4. PASSIONS

The most important characters Antigone, Creon and Haemon, whatever their differences may be, have in common passionate and emotional natures. Antigone speaks so warmly of the dead that her words sometimes sound sinister and perverse. And she is said to be a true descendant of the cursed family of Oedipus: 525-6 'Like father like daughter, passionate, wild'. Creon fails to distinguish law and policy from personal whim and temper so that by the end of the play his hasty judgments are described even by the loyal chorus as 'his own madness ... his own blind wrongs' (1391-2). Haemon is so passionately in love with Antigone that he is unable to remain calm before the attacks Creon makes upon her. In each case the character speaks for an essential part of society (religion and family, government, marriage; see section 6) but seems to undermine his/her case by a lack of self-control. In addition each choral ode dwells at least in part on some aspect of passionate behaviour: battle frenzy (148ff.), the over-bold citizen (413ff.), deluded ambition (690ff.), love (879ff.), anger against the gods (1051ff.), the ecstacies of Dionysus (1239ff.). Sophocles goes beyond what is necessary to make his characters lively and combative (i.e. stage characters rather than philosophers) and seems to insist that we consider not only the issues raised (the rights and wrongs of burial, the ruler's right to rule) but also the issues when promoted by extremists (see section 6).

5. THE GODS

In all Sophocles' plays human beings are powerless before the gods. The gods are great and inscrutable and will overturn human plans made with the best intentions, let alone plans that ignore divine omnipotence. It is not surprising that Creon is proved wrong at the end of the play after his slighting remarks on some of the functions of Zeus (see on 543-6, 735ff.) and his failure to observe basic religious practices. But Zeus is not the only god with an interest. Dionysus, the patron of Thebes, is invoked in the first ode, and in the last, which is a hymn to the god. But in addition to his Theban connection Dionysus is a god of the irrational parts of human life, and his presence reinforces the feeling that the characters are not fully in control of their passions. As does the ode on Aphrodite (879-94) where her effortless power is given great emphasis: 887 'you wrench the minds of the righteous into outrage'. Clearly the difficulties the human characters experience in trying to control their emotions and keep a cool head are reinforced by these gods of the irrational.

6. EXTREMISTS

The chorus sings 'When (man) weaves in the laws of the land, and the justice of the gods that binds his oaths together he and his city rise high' (409-12). The action of the play shows a city in which human laws and divine justice are divided. Antigone defends the right of kinsmen to bury their dead, as sanctioned by the gods and long-established custom. She not only sets this right above the dictates of any government, but ignores the government and state altogether. Creon insists on the supremacy of the state and ignores traditional custom. (He does not ignore the gods, but subsumes their will into the will of the state).

So not only is there conflict, there is also a refusal even to recognise the other's point of view. Between these two extremists the complex structure of a Greek state is divided up, religion and family to Antigone, state to Creon. In practice in classical Athens state and family went closely together: a man became a citizen (and potential holder of office) on the basis of proof of his family background and proof that his family affairs were in order, all established at specific times by religious ceremonies: see on 545. In addition to setting the state against the family, the play also divides the living from the dead, sets men against women, civilisation against nature (see section 8). Furthermore things are put together which should not be: marriage is associated with death, the living are buried alive. By exploiting the grey area over the burial of a traitor, and by peopling his play with passionate fanatics, Sophocles has taken apart Athenian society before the eyes of his Athenian audience.

7. OLD POETRY AND NEW IDEAS

Antigone owes a considerable debt to earlier poetry. The most obvious influence is the *Seven against Thebes* of Aeschylus which told of the preparations for the duel between Eteocles and Polynices. The first ode in *Antigone*, describing the attack on Thebes, recalls Aeschylus, as does the seafaring imagery. On a wider scale the frequent choral comments on the perils of excess and the punishment of boastful words (see e.g. 690ff.) is inherited from Aeschulus and earlier generations of lyric poets who developed the notion of mortals ever striving for more, and suffering under the punishments and restraints imposed by disapproving gods. In many ways Creon's painful learning through suffering is a process familiar from the plays of Aeschylus.

Beside this traditional poetic thought Sophocles places some of the most modern ideas of his own age. This occurs most strikingly in the second ode (376-416) where the progress in civilisation is described in terms borrowed from the philosopher Protagoras, and allusion is made to advances in medicine and to contemporary interests in the development of speech, communications and cities. The ode both pays tribute to the confidence of the age and, in traditional vein, casts doubt on that confidence which so easily veers to overconfidence and destruction. Characters also reflect interests of the 440s when they offer detailed definitions of policical qualities, Creon on leaders at 194ff., Haemon on narrowmindedness at 791ff. The debate between Haemon and Creon (705-878) on government reflects in places contemporary theories of government. The tension between traditional and new thought in the play, like the tensions over burial and women mentioned above, lays bare many of the assumptions and preoccupations of fifth century Athens.

8. POETIC TECHNIQUE

I single out two features. The first is the rich use of themes, often based on imagery, which run through the play. Themes can be traced clearly, but care is needed because implications are not always consistent. For example:

(i) Bird-life. When Creon refuses burial to Polynices birds eat dead human flesh; they no longer give signs to seers; Antigone going about the forbidden burial is compared with a bird. These are signs of bird-life in distress or disorder. But in the first ode we have the metaphor of Polynices' army attacking Thebes like a swooping eagle. Here the bird is powerful and aggressive. And what are we to make of the civilisation ode where on the one hand snaring birds is part of the advance of human civilisation (386), but on the other there are hints that such advance implies human arrogance over the natural world? See notes on 376-416 and 378-85.

(ii) Money. Creon often speaks of money as a corrupter, either literally or in images (see on 335-41), and this might demonstrate his materialistic outlook. But others, Antigone, Haemon and the Chorus, also speak in money terms (e.g. 35,782, 1044).

(iii) Subjugation of nature. Creon sees his role as a subduer of nature (see on 331-2) but metaphors of taming and subjugation are not exculsive to him. Zeus yokes Danae in love at 1040, and at 1051 Dionysus tames Lycurgus with a yoke. One argument from these passages might be that taming humans may be something the gods have a right to do, but to which Creon has no right. But the overall picture may be more ambivalent, again because of the civilisation ode mentioned above on bird-life. In that ode such basic farming practices as taming animals and ploughing are seen on the one hand as signs of cultural improvement and on the other as a potentially dangerous attempt to control nature.

The best discussions of the imagery and themes of the play are in C. Segal *Tragedy and Civilisation* 152-206 and R.F. Goheen *The Imagery of Sophocles' Antigone*.

The second technique to be mentioned is the entrance announcements for new characters on stage. Greek tragedies were given their shape not only by acts and scenes as in the modern conventional theatre but by the choral songs and dances which divided the scenes with actors, and by the arrival of new characters whose entrance was announced by the chorus or a character on stage. In *Antigone* nearly all these entrance announcements are in an animated rhythm. This is extremely unusual, and the animation raises the tempo of the following scene even before it begins. See further on 173-9.

9. THE INFLUENCE OF SOPHOCLES' ANTIGONE
Sophocles' story has been taken up by successive generations of

artists and thinkers, all searching for answers to the conflicts it proposes. I list a few of these works, of which a full description has recently appeared in George Steiner's *Antigones* (Oxford 1984).

In the *Antigone* of Euripides the marriage of Haemon and Antigone, so obliquely dealt with in Sophocles, may have been at the centre of the play. Demosthenes, an Athenian politician of the fourth century BC quotes (19.247) Creon's speech at 194ff. as a model of correct conduct in a politician (which may well lead us to believe that Sophocles intends Creon's early speeches to sound impressive). At the beginning of the last century Sophocles' great conflict between the state and the individual and his themes of family and death had a large influence on some European philosophers, and particularly Hegel. In the twentieth century, the dramatists Anouilh and Brecht adapted Sophocles' play, in each case honouring Antigone as the representative of liberty and the people, and identifying Creon directly or indirectly with the Nazis. These last two examples show how readily the clash between Creon and Antigone can be adapted to any age, but they also perhaps show how well-balanced the original is. Creon may be wrong, but in Sophocles he shares more with Athenian democratic ideals than with the modern totalitarian state.

Notes to Antigone

1-116. Prologue: Antigone appeals to Ismene to join her in burying Polynices.

The darkness before dawn suits the scene of secret plotting (23-4) and gloom, and contributes to the mystery of the first burial of the body (283-316). The contrasting entry of the chorus as it hails the sunrise in a joyful victory ode is striking (see on 117-72). For this dramatic use of darkness and light compare for example the beginning of Aesch. *Agamemnon* and Eur. *Electra*.

1. **My own flesh and blood - dear sister**: Antigone shows warm affection for Ismene, but by the end of the scene (108-10) threatens her with fierce hatred. For Antigone's forceful character see Introduction section 3. Antigone places great emphasis on the bonds and obligations of kinship throughout the play and this lies at the heart of her dispute with Creon. Obligations of kinship also had the greatest significance in the social, political and religious life of Athens, and the conflict in the play lays bare deeply-held beliefs. Whatever the merits of Creon's case against Antigone (and it has its merits, see on 179ff.), it is never seriously disputed that Antigone has on her side both Zeus and the gods of the Underworld: see in particular the notes on 215-35, 499ff., 543-6. Sophocles reinforces Antigone's case by frequent use of words based on *philia* (friendship/family affection/love), *haima* (blood), and with striking rare words: *autadelphon* (very sister/brother) here, 562, 779, *homosplanchnon* (from the same womb) 573.

2. **griefs...handed down**: Antigone and Ismene are the remnants of a cursed family; see Introduction section 2. For Ismene the family history is a reason for taking no action (see 60ff.); Antigone, however, associates honour, kinship, love and religious duty with her dead family (see on 86-92), and beside these associations, which are the mainspring of her actions, love and sisterly affection from Ismene are of little account. This preference for the dead rather than the living is one of the disquieting aspects of Antigone's character. It is also one of the play's ironies that Antigone should stake her life on defending kinship (see note above) in a cursed and polluted family.

5-8. **There's nothing, no pain...**: a series of negative phrases or adjectives is often used in Greek in contexts of lament or regret to make a strong or emotional point; compare 35, note on 963-9, 1190. See Knox.

9. **the Commander**: the choice of word could be sarcastic (compare 37) but need not be.

12-13. **doom reserved for enemies**: Antigone's meaning is not clear. For two suggestions see Knox. The doom referred to is refusal of burial, for which see on 222ff.

23. **past the gates**: tragic characters sometimes go outside the house with all its troubles in order to plot without being overheard (compare Soph. *Electra* 328). Antigone is in effect plotting.

26-36. **Our own brothers' burial**: Antigone describes the discrimination between the brothers in terms of honour given by the rites of burial. Antigone is particularly concerned throughout the play with honour in the sense of public recognition visibly bestowed, and refusal of burial was likely to bring dishonour on the dead man, his kinsmen and the gods of the dead. Polynices 'died miserably' because without burial he was unlikely to be accepted in the Underworld; compare e.g. *Iliad* 23.71 f., 'Bury me quickly so that I may pass the gates of Hades. For the souls, the shades of the dead, keep me at a distance'.

35. **unwept**: at a funeral it was the women's task to weep for the dead (compare Knox Introduction p.39), not alone, but in a group in a formal but emotional lament. The formal lament in tragedy (of which there are examples at 900ff. and 1393ff.) was absorbed into drama from this formal lament in real life.

36. **for birds**: at 229-31 Creon calls the corpse carrion for birds and dogs; but Tiresias shows (1181ff.) that Creon in religious terms has mingled the living of the upper world (and their gods) with the dead of the lower world (and their gods). For the importance of birds in this confusion of the order of things see on 471ff.

44-6. **show what you are...**: Antigone demands visible demonstration of loyalties; compare 100-1. As often in tragedy, demonstration or revelation of the truth behind appearances is important in the play.

57. **for a traitor**: presumably to Polynices.

74-7. **we are women...**: Ismene takes the same view as Creon on the submission of women (see on 593) and on submitting to rulers (see 741ff.). Ismene's conventional thinking highlights the unorthodox social behaviour of Antigone (see further Introduction section 3).

81. **madness**: one of the most prominent features of the play is the stress on states of mind (good sense, folly, passion, madness, good or

bad judgment, etc.), and since states of mind govern processes of thought and action they must be taken into account when rights and wrongs in arguments are being considered. Antigone is called mad or passionate by Ismene, Creon and the chorus on numerous occasions. For 'madness' in Antigone and other characters see Introduction section 4.

86. **death will be a glory**: Antigone is obsessed with the dead, particularly with dead Polynices: she is not merely insisting on a proper burial now (91-2), but on the correct disposition she will have when buried herself (88-90). 'Forever' (90) is a timescale Antigone considers later in discussing the 'unshakable traditions' (505), to be contrasted with Creon's anxiety for the political situation now. Obsession is not too strong a word to use of Antigone:in 87 some critics have noted overtly sexual imagery. Love and honour are also prominent; compare 1 and note. Large questions arise from this obsession with the dead: (i) does Creon deserve more credit if he is defending the world of the living against the sinister Antigone who defends only the other world of the dead? (ii) Can we really believe Antigone loves Haemon as some critics have thought (see on 645-9, in Appendix). (iii) When the time comes for her own death why does Antigone not welcome it? See on 900ff. These questions, especially the first, must be considered in the light both of Sophocles' extreme polarisation of Creon's and Antigone's positions and of their passionate natures (see Introduction sections 4 and 6).

88. **an outrage sacred to the gods**: is defiantly paradoxical: see Knox, and compare the similar 1016 (a passage of religious doubt). Antigone implicitly acknowledges that she does both right and wrong.

102. **it ought to chill your heart**: literally 'you have a hot heart for chilling deeds', chilling because associated with the dead.

108-16. **If you say so...**: the sisters' exchange concludes in the familiar terms of love and (its natural alternative in Antigone's extreme world) hate. 'Leave me to my own absurdity' (111) deserves some thought: is Antigone being ironic or paradoxical, or does she mean that religious truth is not logical and cannot be fully argued for? When we consider Creon's use of rational argument which might be contrasted with religious truth we will find that illogical too; see 499ff. and 705-878. For an excellent discussion of mythical/religious thought and logical thought in the play see C. Segal *Tragedy and civilisation* 161-6.The prologue is a challenge to the audience: is Antigone sane or insane, right or wrong? Does Ismene's partial agreement endorse Antigone's views or make them seem merely extreme (cf. on 74-7)? How do you interpret anything when violent conduct and thought are so interwoven? That question will remain throughout the play.

117-72. *Entry of the chorus and first ode (parodos)*.
See Knox's note. The chorus sing a victory ode, a song describing the defeat of Polynices and the Argives and the happy relief now felt in Thebes. The chorus have a double 'character', first as old men of the city anxious for its safety, and then as commentators on the action of the play who sing in broad poetic terms beyond the limitations of their first 'character'. They sing and they dance. We do not know anything about the choreography, about the relation of dance rhythm to song rhythm or about how singers made complex lyrics comprehensible while they danced.

117. **great beam of the sun**: the sudden blaze of light brings hope; compare Aesch. *Agamemnon* 1-35.

212. **Dirce**: poets readily associate rivers with their cities, principally because of their importance in local myth and religion, such as Inachus at Argos and Cephisus at Athens. Compare 1247 for Thebes' other river, Ismenus, and 1253 for the Castalian spring at Delphi.

122. **white shield**: see Knox for the white shield of Argos (also at 129) and the dragon of Thebes (138).

124. **bridle of fate**: is a (likely) interpretation by scholars, but since the Greek text has only 'bit-and-bridle', the idea of fate is less strong than e.g. at Aesch. *Agamemnon* 217 where Agamemnon is said to put on the 'yoke-strap of necessity' when he accepts the sacrifice of Iphigenia.

125ff....**like an eagle...**: the image of the attacking eagle is a blend of heightened natural detail ('his vast maw gaping') and direct military language (128-31, 134, 139). At 138-9 the eagle grapples with the Theban snake/dragon: Sophocles has taken the traditional enemies eagle and snake (compare *Iliad* 12.200-203) and elaborated them into swooping Argives attacking earth-born Thebans (compare Knox).

140ff. The Argive army is described, and one hero Capaneus, in particular; he was perhaps not named because he was familiar, for example from the *Seven against Thebes* of Aeschylus. Sophocles' language is reminiscent of Aeschylus' play where the attacking army is described as a great wave (cf. 142), the Argives use gold blazons (cf. 143) and Capaneus' shield has the words 'I will burn the city' (cf. 148).

140-1. **Zeus hates...mighty boasts**: the thought is traditional. Zeus' hatred of human pride was incorporated into tragedy from archaic poetry: see Introduction section 7.

149-51. **mad...ecstatic...rage...fury**: Capaneus is specifically called mad, but the eagle-like army is similar (132-9). The chorus believes Thebes has escaped this mad violence but the characters and action of the play prove otherwise: see Introduction section 4.

171. **Lord Dionysus**: for Dionysus and his rites, see on 1239-72.

173-9. **look, the king...is coming...**: it is the usual practice of tragedy to announce a new character before he/she comes on stage (see Introduction section 8). In this play, uniquely in the surviving plays of Sophocles, most entrance-announcements are in a lively rhythm half-way between the lyrics of the odes and the spoken verses of the characters (normally spoken verses are used). Here, and at 417-24 (Antigone), 593-7 (Ismene), 701-4 (Haemon), 895-99 (Antigone) and 1388-92 (Creon), words and rhythm combine to lend an air of anxiety to a new scene.

179-376. *Creon's statement of his beliefs;the sentry's report of the burial of Polynices; Creon's angry response.*

179ff. **My countrymen...** Creon addresses the chorus respectfully (183-8): a ruler needs sound policy (200), and must put his country before all else (203-214). Much of his statement was probably acceptable to the audience (see notes below), though ultimately he is proved wrong (1329ff.). His words here are reassuring to the old Thebans looking for security after the horrors of war. Creon's principal characteristics are anger (first at 317ff.) and a conviction that he is right (e.g. 812ff.); see further Introduction section 3.

180. **the ship of state**: a common metaphor; compare 212, *Oedipus* 27ff., and especially Aesch. *Seven against Thebes* which influenced this play (cf. on 140ff. and 656-6). On sea imagery see on 661-6.

194ff. Supremely ironic lines: Creon's ban on the burial of Polynices (a 'decree' 216, a 'law' 498) leads us to see his lack of judgment and instability of character. It is ironic too that the sentiments of 201 are in accord with Antigone's views at 100-1.

203-4. **friend...country**: the conflict between friend/loved one and the state was a live issue in the fifth century. Euripides wrote a number of plays in which mothers are confronted with the voluntary self-sacrifice of a daughter in the interests of patriotism (e.g. *Children of Heracles, Iphigenia in Aulis*): the most striking example is *Erectheus* where a mother lists reasons for sacrificing her daughter, among them 'We give birth to children for this reason, to defend the altars of the gods and the state'. Thucydides reports the words of Pericles on the tension between state and individual (2.60): 'I believe that when the whole state is on the right footing it benefits the individual more than when each individual is flourishing but the citizen body is in danger. A man may be getting along nicely but if the state is destroyed he too is lost just as much; whereas the individual in misfortune is more likely to pull through when the state prospers.' By 'friend' here and at 209 Creon means his nephew Polynices: he is generalising from his own case, having no notion that his words will apply to a closer friend/relative of Polynices, Antigone.

205. **Zeus my witness**: Creon appeals to Zeus, but his remarks on the gods later change in tone; see on 499ff.

213. **friendships, truer than blood**: see Knox. Creon sees *philia* in a political sense: Athenians regularly used this term of political affiliations between individuals or states, but Creon is (rather alarmingly) putting this sense before the basic sense of kinship relation (see on 1).

215-35. Creon's statement of the different treatment of Eteocles and Polynices, already described by Antigone (26-36), Ismene (67-9), the chorus (160-63) and Creon (189-91) affirmed that the brothers were equal in their desire to kill each other; but Creon now distinguishes the patriot (218) from the traitor (222-6). There could be no objection to that: it is the way he distinguishes the brothers that matters, the granting or refusing of burial without any real interest in the religious implications (see on 222ff., 499ff.).

220. **a hero's honors**: the Greeks honoured the graves of the dead by pouring libations of honey, wine and water to be drunk by the spirits of the dead; see especially *Odyssey* 10.518 and the first scene of Aesch. *Libation Bearers*.

222ff. Antigone as a relative is bound by religion to bury Polynices; but what did the audience think about the burial of traitors, given the general importance of burial (see on 26-36)? We get an idea, at least of common practice, from Thucydides 1.138 (about Themistocles): 'It is said that his relatives brought his bones home as he had instructed and buried him in Attica without the Athenians finding out (for a man exiled for treason could not be buried)'; and Xenophon *Hellenica* 1.7.22: 'Make a judgment if you wish according to the law on temple robbers and traitors: if anyone betrays the city or steals sacred property and at trial is found guilty, he is not to be buried in Attica and his property is to be confiscated.' It looks as if Sophocles is making Creon take the usual view (a city does not bury a traitor in its own soil) to the extreme: Polynices will not be buried at all. See Introduction section 6. (If Knox's interpretation of 12 is right (which is far from certain) Antigone seems to view non-burial in general as acceptable.)

224-5. **gods of his race...**: Polynices is a descendant of Ares (see Knox p 425). For the burning of temples compare Herodotus 8.109 (of Xerxes in Athens): 'He is unholy and reckless because he has made the sacred and profane the same in burning and pulling down the statues of the gods'; cf. Aesch. *Agamemnon* 341ff.

225-6. drink his kinsmen's blood: Polynices was no respecter of kin; cf. on 2n. For the savagery of the phrase compare *Iliad* 24.212-13: Hecabe would eat Achilles' liver if she could. The actual motives of Polynices are of no interest to Sophocles in this play.

236-40. Are the chorus supporting Creon or being guardedly critical? Their tone is uneasy, as it is at 314-6.

248ff. Enter the sentry who reports the token burial of Polynices. He is talkative (cf. 363), and despite the circumstances almost comically irrepressible; he also has a sensible view of human life (see on 264-5). Creon's violent reaction to this character is a prelude to the next scene, and allows us to form a clear picture of him before his confrontation with Antigone.

264-5. I've come...fate: the sentry speaks a truism, but Antigone and Creon do not come to terms with fate until they meet disaster.

277-80. Ritual is satisfied by a token sprinkling of dust.

281. What man: Creon has no notion of a woman doing it; see on 593.

281ff. I've no idea...: Sophocles contrives an air of mystery around the two attempts to bury Polynices, here and at 451ff. (see note there). On this occasion it took place at night (285-6; cf. on 1-116); there is no trace of tools, the sign of human activity; no animal has violated the body (cf. 36, 230) or somehow buried it (293-4). Is this the work of a passer by (see on 291-2), of a guard (295ff.), of a god (314-5) or of Antigone? Antigone must have sprinkled the dust; the mysterious circumstances are intended, if anything, to surround her in an unworldly aura (cf. 464-70).

291-2. The ancient commentary notes: 'Those who saw an unburied corpse and did not scrape up dust over it were thought to be under a curse.' For this peril to passers by compare Horace's striking *Ode* 1.28.

295ff. But what came next!...: the vividness of the dispute is characteristic of a messenger speech.

300. red-hot iron in our fists: this seems to be the only trace of this ordeal in the Greek world. Offering to go through fire is part of the rhetoric of oaths; compare Knox.

314-27. ...the work of the gods...: for the actions of the gods in the burial see on 463ff. Creon's response to the chorus is instructive: (i) his anger is an early sign of a dangerously passionate nature; (ii) charging the chorus with insanity is an example of the ambivalence in the play over states of mind (Creon and Haemon at 705-878); (iii) Creon thinks it is the practice of the gods to reward merit and punish treachery (321-2, 326-7). On Creon's religious beliefs see on 499ff.;

for his attitude to money and rewards see on 335-41.

319-20. It is precisely because Polynices is a corpse that the gods have a concern for him.

324. **golden treasures**: Greek temples were repositories of valuable votive offerings, booty and weapons from successful wars, and state assets. On the impiety of burning temples see on 224-5.

325. **their laws**: the Greek text is unclear: the gods' laws or the laws of the land or both could be intended. Creon believes the laws of the city and the laws of the gods are the same; see on 499ff.

328-35. Creon suspects plots against his rule, and Antigone (564-5) and Haemon (775-84) speak of dissent. Does this suspicion, seen elsewhere in tragic kings (e.g. *Oedipus the King* 406ff.), lead us to regard Creon as a tyrannical ruler as Antigone alleges (566-7), or as a ruler properly alert to the instability in Greek states, especially in the aftermath of war? It is for us, the audience, to decide.

331-2. **tossing wildly...**: in a number of images Creon sees his subjects as animals who are to be subdued: here draught animals to be yoked; 532-3 horses to be broken in; 598 Ismene a viper; 653 animals to be rounded up. In part these relate to other passages where subjects are treated as slaves: 534-5, 581, 824. But there is a link too with the next choral ode (376-416) where human achievement in subduing the natural world is celebrated, though with reservations (see notes).

335-41. **Money!...**:Creon strengthens his charges of bribery with a homily on the dangers of money; he often speaks of money either literally or in images: 247-8, 351-6, 365, 370, 1147-50, 1161, 1171, 1178. But a strong case can be made for taking Creon's language of force (see on 331-2) and money to reinforce the view that his mind is firmly set in this world, in contrast to Antigone's world among the dead and the gods.

346-50. The person who buried the corpse was not a man; 'produce him before my eyes' belongs to the language of revelation, as does 'wring...out of'; but when all is revealed (417ff.) Creon fails to comprehend (see on 528ff.). There is nothing tyrannical in threatening a slave with torture: this was a common way of gathering evidence in the Athenian courts.

376-416. *Choral ode*

In this, perhaps his finest ode, Sophocles blends traditional and modern thought into a remarkable commentary on the play so far, and by implication on contemporary Athens. The main thrust of the ode is a hymn to progress which, like similar passages in tragedy (e.g. Aesch. *Prometheus Bound* 442-506 and Eur. *Suppliant Women* 195-215) probably derives from *On the original state of things*, a work by the philosopher Protagoras of Abdera which only survives in Plato's version in *Protagoras* 320-322. The general belief in improvement in the human condition, culminating in the Greek city state, shows a confidence in human society and achievements. Sophocles' ode goes further in attributing improvement not to a kindly god (usually Prometheus) but to mankind alone (compare the philosopher Xenophanes: 'The gods did not reveal everything to men in the beginning; men improved things gradually with enquiry.') Against this optimistic modern account of life Sophocles introduces traditional poetic reflections on the dangers of ambition and success and the inevitability of death. For the blend of old and new, and, at least partial, dissent from fifth century confidence see Introduction sections 7-8.

The dramatic context of the choral ode is as follows. The chorus is anxious: having witnessed a scene in which their hopes have been set back by an unexplained act of defiance in which the gods may have a hand, they introduce their praise of man with 'numberless wonders, terrible wonders'. Immediately after the ode they are confronted with 'a dark sign from the gods' (417). In this uneasy setting the ode itself becomes ambivalent: man is 'skilled, the brilliant' (390); he has 'thought quick as the wind' (395) and 'mood and mind for law' (396); he is 'ready, resourceful' (401); 'he has plotted his escapes' (405). These are faculties of the mind. Is man really as much in control here as he appears? 'All these he has taught himself' (397); later in the play hard lessons are taught to man (see on 1470). Can we be confident in what he teaches himself here? In the first two stanzas man subdues nature to his own use: can we wholeheartedly approve of this triumph over the natural world when Creon by subjugating humans (part of the natural word) becomes a tyrant (see on 331-2)? For the relevance of the ode to Antigone and Creon see on 406-16.

376-7. A (deliberate?) echo of Aesch. *Libation Bearers* 572f., also the beginning of a choral ode, on the violence of women. An ironic reminiscence by Sophocles, for a woman as the criminal is a 'terrible wonder' not considered by the chorus (cf. 417ff.).

378-85. The first achievements considered are over the forces of nature. The sea, usually a hostile dangerous force in ancient literature, is a challenge to the enterprising man; on the significance of the sea in the play see on 661-6. The earth is subdued to the plough. At first there seems no comparison between the boldness man needs to plough the earth and the audacity needed to tackle the sea at its most violent ('the blasts of winter' are the southerly gales which blow up the Aegean). But the earth here is seen as the oldest of the gods, 'the immortal, the inexhaustible'. Although man must plough he should remember this. Perhaps there is a link with Creon's presumption in placing a living person *in the earth* and denying the gods under the earth the corpse which is their due (see especially 1185-90)?

386-94. Man controls wild beasts, snaring them in air, land and sea, or yoking them however wild the terrain.

405. from desperate plagues: medicine was in the forefront of scientific advance in the fifth century. Consider for example the confidence of Hippocrates *On Ancient Medicine* 2: 'For a long time medicine has had everything, and has discovered a principle and method by which many good discoveries have been made over the years; and everything else will be discovered if the researcher is up to it.'

406-16. Man the master...: what was hinted in the earlier stanzas is now expressed: if man is too ingenious he loses control, the unpredictable takes over. Sophocles is moving the thought of the ode towards the moralising tradition where gods and fate act against human ambition. Gods are only mentioned obliquely in this stanza (410) but the traditional thought is clear in 'past all dreams', 'weds himself to inhumanity', 'reckless daring'.

410-6. the laws of the land...: the chorus are generalising since they do not know who has disobeyed Creon: they are prescribing proper conduct for the individual in the city-state. But the conflict in the play arises because Creon (however politically correct he may be) contravenes a basic stipulation of the gods (the dead must be buried), and Antigone (whatever her religious justification) flouts a law of the land. The audience is entitled to ask, to whom do these words better apply? The answer could be Creon, for Antigone's action, a ritual performed from the earliest times, can hardly be called 'past all dreams' or an action of 'inhumanity' even if the circumstances give rise to 'reckless daring'. Sophocles has set his ode, apparently to comment on the terrible action of the law-breaker (see on 376-416), but to include possible criticism of Creon. This pattern reappears in subsequent odes.

412-3. 'He and his city rise high' contrasts with its negative 'but the city casts out' in exactly the same place in the stanza as in the last 'resourceful man' contrasts with 'never without resources'. For a similar effect of echo compare 689 and 700.

415. share my hearth: the family gods guarded the hearth of a house and were worshipped there. For the exclusion of a criminal from this sensitive place compare *Oedipus the King* 272-87. The Greeks thought it unwise in general to associate with criminals, even to travel on the same boat, in case they suffered the gods' punishment as well as the guilty.

417-24. Here is a dark sign...: the chorus in alarm see Antigone approaching. They speak in animated rhythm (see on 173-9); they again suspect divine intervention (cf. 315-6); they see that the troubles in the family of Oedipus are not yet over; they suppose Antigone has acted madly (see on 81), very like the man of reckless daring from whom they have just dissociated themselves (415-6).

425-655. *The sentry reports how Antigone buried Polynices; Antigone makes a statement of belief, to which Creon reacts with hostility. Their lengthy argument, in which Ismene later joins, concludes with Creon confirming the death sentence on Antigone.*

451 ff. The sentry describes the second token burial of Polynices, for the covering of dust has been swept away (453). The first burial occurred in mysterious circumstances (see on 281ff.) but on this occasion the guards are fully alert: (i) the exact condition of the body is known (454); (ii) the guards select a vantage point (455); (iii) they keep themselves on their toes before, not after, the crime (457-9, contrast 295ff.); (iv) the day is at its hottest and brightest (460-2). Nevertheless when the second burial is about to take place, an air of mystery returns (see on 463ff.).

454. it was slimy, going soft: the words are disturbing, as were Antigone's at 36 and Creon's at 230. For the implications of flesh in which the gods have an interest (here a human corpse) becoming slimy see on 1110ff.

455. For the location of Polynices' body in the Theban plain see on 1319. We should imagine either a hill to one side which happens to be underwind or, more likely, higher ground on two or three sides of the corpse, with the guards choosing a side that is underwind.

463ff. A whirlwind comes from nowhere, shrouding in mystery Antigone's arrival at the corpse. It does not conceal her second burial of Polynices (474ff.); rather, it associates her with the religious forces that Creon has disturbed. The dust-storm is 'a black plague of the heavens', but it is not clear whether the heavens sent the plague or are suffering from it. The gods certainly play a part (468) but what is most emphasised is the confusion and blending of earth and heaven (and by implication, confusion of the preserves of the gods of the upper world and the gods of the dead). Creon's later actions against Antigone compound the confusion as Tiresias explains at 1185-90. We cannot say precisely how the whirlwind, religious forces and Antigone are associated, but Antigone herself does not fully understand the way the gods act (see on 1013-21). All we can say is that Antigone is somehow part of the world of the dead (see on 86) and of the order that the gods preside over for ever (see on 499ff.).

471ff....**like a bird**...: bird similes are common in tragedy: one of the best-known is the simile of the vultures robbed of their young at Aesch. *Agamemnon* 54ff. In this play Sophocles makes a telling connection between birds and the corpse. Polynices is left for birds to scavenge from, in Antigone's ironically lush words 'a lovely treasure for birds that scan the field and feast to their heart's content; (35-6). Creon's words make clear the outrage done to the body: 'carrion for the birds...an obscenity' (230-1). But the full, religious scale of the outrage is shown by the prophetic birds of Tiresias: 'a strange voice in the wing-beats, unintelligible, barbaric, a mad scream! Talons flashing, ripping, they were killing each other - that much I knew - the murderous fury whirring in those wings made that much clear!' (1106-1110). Here at 471, Antigone's cry of distress is like that of a bird. Sophocles evidently used birds in this way in the play because of their importance in giving signs from the gods to seers. We should note, finally, that the army of Polynices was like a bird, albeit an aggressive one, when it attacked Thebes (127ff.). For sequences of association, literal and metaphorical, of this kind see Introduction section 8.

481. **like hunters**: the image reinforces the idea of Creon and his agents hunting or subduing animals and birds, which are associated with religious forces (see previous note).

499ff. At her first meeting with Creon, Antigone distinguishes between the 'great unwritten unshakable traditions' presided over by Zeus and the Justice dwelling with the nether gods, and Creon's edict on Polynices. She does not challenge Creon's right to make edicts (or laws or proclamations); in fact she has no interest in how the city is governed (see below) except where Creon does violence to past traditions, and in particular the tradition of burial. For his part, Creon has no interest in traditions, merely in his right to govern absolutely. Henceforth Creon is on dangerous ground in two respects: (i) Greek states, including Athens, were conservative over traditional beliefs; compare Pericles in the Funeral Speech (Thucydides 2.37), 'We do not infringe...(those laws)... which are unwritten and which bring shame recognised by all (on the transgressor).' (ii) The gods. Hitherto nearly all Antigone's appeals have been to the nether gods; now she includes Zeus. Creon does not challenge her: for him the gods can be taken for granted as part of the state (180, 205-6, 224, 316ff., 345), and anyone who makes grand statements about them is a fanatic. Consequently his references to the gods degenerate into sarcastic jibes at Antigone's faith (545, 736). Creon replies to Antigone's speech at 528-554, but, unlike many of Euripides' plays where one speech answers the other point by point, there is no contact between them on the vital principle that divides them. Creon in his speech does not comment on the ultimate authority of the gods; and Creon's claim to authority is not tested until his scene with Haemon.

499-501. **Zeus...that Justice**: Greek gods had a variety of spheres of influence: Antigone is presumably thinking of Zeus in his aspect of a god of the dead. 'That Justice' is, equally, a personification of a particular part of justice, or the right order of things, namely the requirement that the underworld gods lay on the living to bury the dead.

505. **unwritten...traditions**: unwritten laws, that is custom, the law of nature and moral justice were discussed by the fourth century philosophers; see Plato *Laws* 793a, Aristotle *Nichomachean Ethics* 1180bl, 1162b22.

506. **They are alive**: for the laws of the gods as living things compare *Oedipus the King* 957, 'Great laws tower above us...never lost in sleep.' The laws of the gods 'live forever': Antigone's words match the eternal timescale of the gods (see on 677-686) with her own commitment to eternity (see on 86).

510. **wounded pride**: Antigone reduces Creon's motives to wounded pride, as he ignores her religious claims and concentrates on her 'insolence' (536ff.).

512-20. **Die I must...**: Antigone remains as little interested in her mortal life as in the prologue. Tragic heroines facing a great challenge commonly put a small value on their unhappy life: compare Soph. *Electra* 959ff., Eur. *Hecuba* 349ff. For the contrasting sentiments later expressed by Antigone, also characteristic of tragic heroines facing death, see on 900ff.

524. **folly**: religious devotion was as easily censured as folly in the fifth century (see Eur. *Bacchae*) as in the time of St Paul (*1 Corinthians* 1.18f). But, more important, the gulf between Antigone and Creon is again expressed in terms of passion or states of mind.

526. **passionate, wild**: note the words of the chorus: they criticise the passion of Antigone sooner than the anger of Creon, and continue so doing until she goes to her death (see 1022-3). Outside the choral odes the chorus speak as loyal Theban subjects (see on 117-72) who are remarkably uncritical of the king until he breaks down (1221f.), though within the odes matters are more ambivalent (see on 410-16).

528ff. Creon in his answering speech introduces a general reflection on stubbornness (528-35) before speaking on Antigone in particular. The lack of contact between them is reinforced by Creon's speaking of Antigone to the chorus rather than to her direct. To the language of subjugation and slavery (see on 331-2) Creon adds a comparison with iron-making.

536-40. insolence: this passage well illustrates what a Greek meant by *hybris*, a term covering both a wanton or insolent action, and the state of mind that gives rise to or accompanies that action. Compare the amusing incident in Demosthenes 54.8-9 where a man is knocked down in the street (an act of *hybris*) and seeks to prove *hybris* in the minds of his attackers by the report that they stood over him crowing and flapping their arms like a victorious cock. For Antigone overriding the edicts see on 677-686, for the sensibility of the Greeks to laughter see on 930.

541. she is the man: for the conflict between men and women in the play see on 593.

543-6. Creon is carried away by his rhetoric: not only do his words set him at variance with Antigone (for kinship and blood see on 1, for Zeus see on 499ff.), but they almost certainly sounded sinister to the audience. Creon is defending the state, but his view of the state is one where the unwritten traditions appear not to be recognised (see on 499ff.), where kinship is spoken of lightly (in Athens a man's civic and political rights depended on his family and kinship group), and where the altar of Zeus has no sanction. See further on 735ff.

545. Guardian Zeus: literally 'Zeus of the Courtyard' i.e. in his aspect of god of the household. Consider Aristotle's list of questions asked of intending officials in Athens (*Constitution of the Athenians* 55.3): 'Who is your father and which deme is he from? Who is your father's father and who your mother and who is your mother's father and which deme is he from? ...Does the man have an ancestral Apollo and a courtyard Zeus, and where are their shrines?'

549. hysterical: the audience must judge the accuracy of this judgement of Ismene. In terms of the themes of the play Creon says she is of unsound mind, 'up to no good, plotting' (551f.) and plotting 'in the dark' (see on 1-116).

558-62. Then why delay? ...: Antigone is not only inflexible but makes no attempt at argument, being satisfied that 'I know I please where I must please the most' (i.e. the dead), 103. Contrast Haemon who attempts to make contact with his father in the speech 764-809, addressing him (764, 784) and urging a different line of action (804). For Antigone's association of glory with the dead see on 86.

563. citizens...would all agree: for possible dissent among the chorus and citizens see on 236-40 and 328-35.

568-649. Speeches are replaced by rapid exchanges between characters ('stichomythia'), between Creon and Antigone, Ismene and Antigone, and Ismene and Creon. The function of stichomythia is to precipitate a decision (e.g. 49ff.), to convey information quickly (e.g. 443ff.) or, as here, to confirm an impasse reached in longer speeches.

At the end of each of the three sections of stichomythia here (591-2, 630-1, 649) it is affirmed that Antigone will die.

573. **my own flesh and blood**: literally 'from the same womb'. For Antigone's striking affirmations of kinship see on 1.

575. **the same mother, the same father**: for Antigone significant relations are fixed from birth: Polynices and Eteocles are brothers and that overrides all else. For Creon, relationships are made, and change with circumstances, especially political circumstances (compare 212-3).

586-9. **the ones below...death**: the attitude of the dead in this matter may be a moot point. In the Underworld scene in *Odyssey* 11, Ajax is unwilling to speak to Odysseus because of a grudge he carried to the grave (543ff.).

590. On this striking line see Knox.

591. **Go down below and love**: Creon appears to accept Antigone's claims to represent not only the wishes of the dead but also the bonds of *philia* (love/affection/kinship, see on 1), about which he had earlier spoken lightly (see on 543-6). His unfortunate punishment, when it comes, will be the death of those he holds dear, his wife and son.

593. **no woman**: Creon makes a series of comments hostile to women: 541-2 'I am not the man...she is the man if this victory goes to her'; 593 'no woman is going to lord it over me'; 652 'from now on they'll act like women'; 723 'never lose your sense of judgment over a woman'; 758ff. 'never let some woman triumph over us'; 828 'the woman's side'; 836f. 'you...woman's accomplice'; 848 'you woman's slave'. I do not think it possible to speak of a *conflict* between men and women in the play because Creon's words are not picked up or commented on by others. Sexual conflict is certainly a common theme in tragedy, seen at its strongest in the *Oresteia* of Aeschylus where women's violence is shown to undermine (male) civilisation. But in *Antigone* the underlying fabric of society is upheld by Antigone (see e.g. on 499ff. and 543-6). Ismene's timid remark 'Remember we are women, we're not born to contend with men' (74-5) reflects orthodox fifth century thought and could be taken to support Creon's remarks (see note there) but the rest of the play does not bear it out. Nor is it possible to link the dangers of passion specifically with women, for the strongest passions in the play are seen in Haemon, and the necessity for Creon to recognise the errors to which his own passions have led him is of central importance in the final scenes. It is probably best to link Creon's remarks on women with those on other subversives (e.g. 328-32) who, like high-spirited animals, must have their spirit tamed (see on 331-2). At 642 Creon speaks of women in another natural

image, that of arable land; see note there for the implications of the metaphor. In dismissing women Creon by implication dismisses sexual love and kinship; for sexual love see on 879-94, for kinship see on 1. For speculation on a wiser use of sexual oppositions in the play to reflect Greek beliefs on parenthood and changes in Athenian society see C. Segal *Tragedy and Civilisation* 183-6.

603-31. The second section of the long sequence of stichomythia. Ismene and Antigone are together for the first time since the prologue. Ismene was invited to share in the burial (50) but refused; now that the deed is done Antigone will allow no sharing (604ff., 615, 625). She with her brothers will share love (590) in one world; Ismene is in the other world, of the living (626, 628).

628. **Your wisdom**: Antigone distinguishes between wisdom among the living and wisdom among the dead. Most criticism of her state of mind in the play fails to take this into account (see on 81 and 526); for reasons see on 900ff.

634-50. The third section of stichomythia.

642. **fields for him to plough**: the image of ploughing for sexual intercourse is common; compare *Women of Trachis* 32f. (Heracles rarely sees his wife) 'like a farmer who takes on a distant field of ploughing land and sees it only at seedtime and harvest'; *Oedipus the King* 1626 'I fathered you in the soil that gave you life.' But Creon's tone is harsh, and thematically linked with the ambiguous words of the chorus on farming (see on 378-85).

648. **Death will do it**: Antigone's intended marriage to Haemon was first mentioned at 641. Creon is the first to connect marriage with death; at 730 he says she can find a husband among the dead, thus anticipating Antigone's vision of herself as the bride of Death in her lament. See on 900ff.

651-3. **Take them in...**: Creon speaks in (male) fifth century terms: women should remain indoors out of sight (see e.g. Thucydides 2.45). For the image of women as animals to be tied up see on 593.

656-700. *A choral ode in lyrics in two pairs of stanzas.*

In contrast with the last ode (see on 376-416) the thought is traditional. The gods punish the sins of a house from generation to generation, leading men on to destruction. The first two stanzas echo Aeschylus in particular: some houses are doomed (656-66), and the particular family considered is the house of Oedipus (666-77). The last two stanzas contrast the permanence of the law of Zeus (677-86) with the precariousness of human fortunes. Also contrasted are 'the dazzling crystal mansions of Olympus' (684) and ruin for men 'like a...tide...surging over the dead black depths' (661-3). The pessimistic tone derives from the death sentence just confirmed on Antigone, but the ode has a wider reference to her and Creon; see on 686-700.

656. **Blest**: Greek poets sometimes praise the blessed as a prelude to thoughts on unhappiness; compare Bacchylides 5.50ff. 'Blessed is he to whom god has given a share of good things...for no mortal is entirely fortunate.'

661-6. **a great mounting tide...**: the sea as a metaphor of human misfortune is a commonplace: it has rich associations in *Antigone*. The first is a debt to the *Seven against Thebes* of Aeschylus (which shows an earlier stage in the fight between Eteocles and Polynices): Eteocles is frequently seen as the helmsman trying to guide the ship of state over dangerous seas. Consider next the details of the remarkably vivid description of an Aegean storm that Sophocles has given: the sea is driven 'by savage northern gales'; there is relentless movement ('surging', 'roiling up'); there is darkness in the depths which the sea brings to the surface. For Greeks the north is Thrace, a source not just of storm winds but also of savage passions (see on 1053, 1066ff.). The movement of the sea reflects the movement or unpredictability in human affairs mentioned by the chorus at 406ff. and 689ff. Darkness in the play has sinister implications; see on 1-116. Such is the metaphorical sea which the chorus showed man crossing in the last ode (see on 378-85, and compare note on 376-416) and over which Creon believes he can guide the ship of state safely (180-2, 212). The dangers Creon runs are spelt out by Haemon who explicitly links the king's passionate nature with his attempt to sail difficult seas (see 794ff.).

666-77. The chorus set out in traditional religious terms the troubles of the family, already alluded to by Antigone, Ismene and the chorus theselves (see on 2, 526). The pattern of inherited sorrow in a family, described in 666-72, is most powerfully illustrated in tragedy in the *Agamemnon* of Aeschylus where the apparently innocent (Iphigenia) and the apparently guilty (Agamemnon) meet their deaths in the gods' complex pursuit of the crimes of ancestors.

677-86. In contrast to men, Zeus' power is invincible and unchanging. While human houses are rocked to the foundations (658) and brought crashing down by external forces ('the gods', 'some god') Zeus, impervious to all force, holds fast his crystal mansions (684). Despite the great gulf between Zeus and men there are always those who try to make inroads on Zeus' power, who try to override it (678-9). Who are the chorus thinking of? Antigone, who has been charged with overriding human edicts (537) or Creon? See on 686-700ff. Zeus and his laws were uniquely resistant to sleep; see in particular *Oedipus the King* 952-62 (quoted at note on 505f). Sleep, time and age frequently appear as forces that restrict mortals (as opposed to gods). For the changes wrought by time compare *Oedipus at Colonus* 686ff. The chorus now introduce one of the eternal laws of Zeus.

686-700. The law is the traditional one, that excess makes ruin likely. While at 406-16 ingenuity brought unpredictable fortunes, excess here brings disaster that is all too predictable, reinforced by the echo of 689 in 700. There is further reminiscence of 406-16, though in more pessimistic vein, in the dwelling on states of mind. But the new element here is the stress on delusion that is sent by the gods. Hopes, linked ominously with an image of the sea (see on 661-6), lead to a loss of mental control: where man in the earlier ode at least appeared to control the physical world (see on 376-416), here he is the unwitting victim.

The lesson 'foul is fair, fair is foul to the man the gods will ruin' is said to be 'famous' and so well known that its author is forgotten (695). What if anything is the application of this 'famous saying' to the play? The many terms for mental instability lead us to think first of Antigone whom the chorus called passionate and wild, but it is hard to see how insistence on religious law could be seen as a confusion of 'fair with foul' or a 'fraud' stealing on her slowly. Nor does she make any claim to greatness. As in the last ode the chorus seems, rather, to be speaking of Creon. His is the power and greatness (Antigone spoke of his power and tyranny at 566-7); his are the sinister words about Zeus and kinship (543-6). Is it he who is 'unaware till he trips'? Compare note on 410-16.

700. **blinding ruin**: *atē* in Greek has broadly two meanings: 'bewilderment' or 'delusion' sent by the gods, usually in punishment for human excesses; and the 'ruin' which the unbalanced sufferer brings upon himself. Ruin is the dominant sense in Sophocles (e.g. in this ode at 659, 689, 700), but 697-8 clearly marks an assault on a man's mind by the gods. Fagles has brought this out in his translation 'blinding ruin'. For the notion of both a state of mind and its consequence in *ate* compare the similar notions in *hybris* (see on 536-40).

701-4. **Here's Haemon now**: Haemon is introduced in animated rhythm (see on 173-9). Before he speaks a word it is suggested that he may be distressed and resentful.

705-878. *Creon and Haemon clash over Antigone.*

The question of marriage has only recently entered the play (641ff.) but introduces a vital new element: it links Haemon closely to Antigone; it causes Antigone's tone to change and her position to become more complex (see on 900ff); and it adds sexual love to the play's other passions (see on 879-94). The scene is structurally similar to the last: two long speeches lead to an irreconcilable clash in stichomythia (see on 568-649).

707-8. **raving against your father**: Creon identifies opposition as mental instability as did he and the chorus in the case of Antigone and Ismene (see 525-7, 632-4). He now takes love (*philia*; see on 1), which he earlier defined as patriotic solidarity (see on 213), a stage further: 'Do you love me, no matter what I do?' See on 746-51.

709-12. Haemon's words appear at first calm and conciliatory. But there is an ambiguity in the Greek as Knox points out, and Haemon might be saying 'you, when you are wise...' (709) and 'if you give good direction' (712).

714. **subordinate**: Creon earlier defined power in imagery drawn from the subjugation of nature (see on 331-2). In this speech the dominant imagery is military; for the implications see on 741-5.

715ff. **to produce good sons...**: Creon's general remarks on fathers and sons, while apparently reflecting the high value Athenians placed on family solidarity, seem in fact to exaggerate the father's role. This impression is confirmed at 735ff. (see note). Having the same friends and enemies is a standard expression of solidarity both on a personal level and in relations between states.

721. **mockery**: the Greeks were sensitive to laughter; see on 930ff.

723ff. **never lose your...judgement over a woman...**: there are many general reflections in tragedy on the dangers of bad women (perhaps not surprising since playwrights and probably audience - though this is disputed - were all men): compare e.g. Eur. *Hippolytus* 616 'O Zeus, why did you bring that false coin, woman, into the sun's light?', Eur. *Andromache* 272 'No one has yet found a cure for a bad woman.' Other reflections are more balanced: Soph. fragment 682 'A man has no worse possession than a bad woman, and no better than a good one,' Eur. fragment 494 'There is nothing more evil than a bad woman, and absolutely nothing better than a good one.' Note Creon's strong language: for spitting see on 1359, for Antigone's wedding in the Underworld see on 900ff.

735ff. **let her cry for mercy...**: Creon again speaks lightly of Zeus' protection of families (compare note on 543-6), thereby casting a sinister shadow on what follows. The argument is reasonable up to a point: a house should be well-run, and so should a state (note that 739-40 mean literally 'whoever is a good man in his home affairs will prove just in the city also': Fagles wrongly stresses the notion of rule). And for practical purposes the military analogy holds good. But Creon is being challenged on fundamental religious obligations (burial of the dead) and in placing too little value on Zeus, kindred blood and right and wrong (751) he comes perilously close to the criminal of the last ode who failed to distinguish fair from foul (696-8).

741-5. **comrade at your side**: the heavily-armed Greek armies of the fifth century (hoplites) depended on close formation in battle. Creon's use of the military image helps him to stress the willing obedience of the individual which was not present in the earlier imagery of subjugation (see on 714).

746-51. Creon's arguments about loyal sons (715ff.) and military discipline stressed the role of the father and commander, leading to the individual ruler here. His reasoning not only fails to take account of how all suffer if the one leader is wrong (bad tactics in battle, for example) but explicitly rejects questions of right and wrong (751; cf. 708, 714, and note on 735ff.).

751-61. **Anarchy...**: Creon recapitulates with a general denunciation of anarchy, leading to a somewhat incoherent attack on Antigone at 757ff. Is the suggestion that women are more likely to break the law? For women see on 593.

761-3. Whatever unease Creon's words arouse in the audience, the chorus (outside the odes) are loyal in their support. See 900ff. for the dramatic advantages of this.

770-84. Haemon reports (and we have no reason to disbelieve him) that the citizens, unlike the chorus (see previous note), regard the burial in the way Antigone does. They are said to call her action glorious; they use Antigone's term *autadelphon* (779) for the brother/sister relationship (see on 1); and they share her revulsion for the exposing of a body. Haemon twice says these words are spoken in the dark (see on 1-116); we are at liberty to interpret them as the rebellious words of dissidents (cf. 328ff.) or as words spoken in fear of a tyrannical ruler. The context leads us to favour the latter (cf. 821ff.).

788-809. **Now don't please...**: Haemon, who was introduced as a man liable to anger (704, 707) and who rushes distraught from the stage (859), attempts to make contact with his father in a calm and rational manner (see on 558-62 for the lack of contact between Antigone and Creon). Haemon does not answer Creon's political points, but appeals to him to yield (804). Sophocles often created characters who take a firm, determined stand and refuse to change their mind despite adverse conditions: examples are Ajax, Electra, Oedipus, Philoctetes, and Antigone at the beginning of the play. A refusal to change is then a characteristic quality of Sophocles' heroes, and if a change does occur, as with Neoptolemus in *Philoctetes* or Creon later in *Antigone* (see on 1218-21), that moment is most significant. Failure to yield often leads to destruction, but the audience may be led to feel that a heroic stand is in some way justified. In this play however there are special circumstances: a particular stress on states of mind at all times (and obstinacy is of course a state of mind) and in addition a growing suspicion that Creon's stance is wrong (see e.g. on 735ff.). In dramatic terms, Haemon's speech and the following stichomythia mark an exciting point in the plot: will Creon retract the death sentence before it is too late?

Apart from Antigone, Haemon is the first to criticise Creon's mental state. It is for the audience to decide whether these are the words of a madman or the voice of reason (see Introduction paragraph 4).

794ff. **No, it's no disgrace...**: for learning see on 1470. The illustration of the tree standing in the raging torrent and the sailor in difficulty at sea could be drawn from Sophocles' own observation, or (more likely) from earlier poetry. See for example *Iliad* 5.87-92 for the simile of a torrent. For the nautical image see on 661-6.

810-14. **You'd do well, my lord...**: Creon's refusal to yield (see 788-804) is linked to a refusal to learn or even listen. When he gives way he gives way on both; see 1218ff. His objection to learning from a younger man is then a side issue. For the sentiment compare Menander fragment *638* 'Don't look at it as me speaking as a young man, but as whether my words are the words of the wise.'

817. **rebels**: compare 737 and the converse in 757.

819. **sickness**: for the theme of disease in the play see on 1123.

821-7. **And is Thebes to tell me...**: the sequence of stichomythia drives Creon to extremes. It is in theory reasonable for the king to retain the right to rule (821), though many Athenians may not have thought so; compare Aristotle *Politics* 1287a 'On the subject of absolute kingship so-called (that in which the king rules totally, in accord with his own wishes), some think it unnatural that one man should have power over all citizens where the city is composed of equals.' And the play encourages us to ask, what if the absolute ruler is wrong in his wishes (cf. on 746-51)? Creon's next line (823) is ambiguous and could mean 'Am I to rule this land as others see fit or as I see fit?' But Haemon takes it in the sense '...for the profit of others or my own profit?' (824), and Creon endorses this meaning in 825 'The city *is* the king's.' We might recall Creon's earlier language of subjugation and financial possession (see on 331-2 and 335-41).

827-30. **the woman's side**: Creon's opposition to Antigone as a woman remains slightly puzzling (see on 593). Haemon's reply perhaps means that a woman is a suitable recipient for the consideration he is showing his father. These lines do not exactly follow the argument of the preceding lines, but this is a common occurence in stichomythia. Compare 586-593, and next note.

835. you trample down: trampling or kicking the things of the gods are traditional acts of impiety; see on 943-6. Haemon confronts Creon in a way the chorus failed to do; see further on 900ff. Creon again avoids the challenge by another sexual jibe.

837-8. accomplice: in both lines this word is a mistranslation: read 'inferior to a woman' and 'you'll never find me giving in to foul deeds.' In the male-oriented Greek value system domination over inferiors (of which women were one) was expected; compare 848.

841. And you, and me...: Haemon recalls Antigone in refusing to divide kinsman from kinsman or living from dead.

843. another: Haemon means himself; Creon takes it as a threat against himself.

845-6. mindless judgments: for mutual and unproductive charges of stupidity see on 510 and 524. More alarmingly, the exchange ends at 858 with Haemon 'in a burst of anger' charging Creon with 'rage' (in Greek the word is madness). If earlier scenes have portrayed various states of mind, this one shows greater extremes than any. For the significance of this see on 879-94 and 900ff.

861. a temper young as his: the chorus, as guarded as ever, link passion with youth (in part rightly; see on 879-94) but fail again to make the obvious comments about Creon.

863. something desperate: a line of tragic irony: what Haemon dreams up is all too human; it is Creon who has gone beyond his human limitations, identifying himself with the criminal of the last ode (686-700, with notes), and committing grave religious crimes (see 1185-90).

866. you really intend...?: the first time the chorus seriously challenge Creon; and they save Ismene's life. Compare their crucial role at 1214ff.

870-8. I'll take her down...: the punishment originally specified for burying Polynices was stoning to death (see 43). Why does Creon change the sentence? The change implies a shift from death inflicted by the whole community against a religious felon to a private death in which the executioner himself takes precautions against defilement. (See Knox's note.) Taking a life could be a complex undertaking in Greek cities for there was a danger of divine retribution. Creon here tries to avoid the guilt for starving Antigone to death (872-3: Fagles' 'just the measure piety demands' is an insensitive translation. Read 'set out rations sufficient to absolve us of guilt, to keep...'). For the perils he runs consider for example the following case (Thucydides 1.134): King Pausanias of Sparta sought sanctuary in a temple of Athena; the Spartans took off the roof and bricked up the doors to starve him out; they took the precaution to remove him from holy ground before he died; but Apollo was nevertheless angry and declared their actions brought pollution on them. Why does Creon take such a risk? We can speculate that his preference for private punishment is a tacit admission that the city is against him (cf. 773ff.) or that he is now so enraged against Antigone that he devises for her the worst death he can imagine. But the significance of these lines lies beyond such speculations:

(i) In 876 Creon speaks lightly of death and in 878 says 'what a waste of breath it is to revere the things in the house of Hades' (I translate the end of the line literally, for Fagles' 'Death' omits the dead themselves who are also included). These words are as sinister as his levity about Zeus (see on 543-6 and 735ff.).

(ii) 'Wall her up alive' (871) introduces the notion of a living death for Antigone, a major theme of her lament (see 900ff.).

(iii) Creon has the last word in a scene in which marriage (730), kinship (735-6), government (821-7), and even death (see (i) above) have been spoken of in a most disturbing way. Creon, who has full executive powers, is to be punished (1181ff.); but what will Antigone's response be? See on 900ff.

879-94. *A choral ode in one pair of lyrical stanzas on the power of sexual love.*

For other poetic treatments of this theme see e.g. Sappho fragment 1, Eur. *Medea* 627ff., Eur. *Hippolytus* 525-64. For the portrayal of Aphrodite at her most powerful in Sophocles see *Women of Trachis* 497-530 and R.P. Winnington-Ingram *Sophocles, An Interpretation* 91ff. Love (Eros) is the personification of sexual passion and rarely appears as a full god in myth or religious cult; but he is frequently given the attributes of Aphrodite, the goddess of love, of whom he is the constant companion (see below). The ode is ostensibly a choral comment on the emotions aroused in Haemon in the previous scene by the death sentence on Antigone. Sophocles has given us much food for thought: in delaying explicit mention of love until now, Sophocles made Haemon speak to Creon on the problems at issue, kinship, the gods, government etc. But we are bound to wonder how far all of Haemon's words were coloured by his love for his doomed bride.

Wider issues are also raised in this ode. Passion of one kind or another has been mentioned in each of the earlier odes (see on 149-51, 410-16 and 686-700), usually as a bad, or at least a dangerous force; and in the last two cases there was good reason for thinking that Creon's nature was under consideration. Here the passion of love, whether good or bad, is shown to be universal, affecting even the gods (884), and irresistible. It is, then, disturbing that Creon has tried to thwart love in the previous scene (see Knox); see on 870-8 section (iii) for the forces against which Creon has already set himself. And it seems that 887-90 must refer as much to Creon's state of mind as to Haemon's. The ode also overshadows Antigone's lament which follows (see on 900ff. and 905-8).

879. **never conquered in battle**: compare Plato *Symposium* 196d 'as regards courage, Ares cannot withstand Love, for Ares is not the master of Love but Love of Ares.' See 893.

881. **standing the night-watch**: the metaphor appears to be unparalleled in Greek.

882. **a girl's soft cheek**: compare Phrynichus (the tragic poet) fragment 13 'The light of love shines on rosy cheeks.' Greek poetry seems rarely to have associated desire with cheeks, commonly with eyes (see 891). The girl is mentioned in a context of battle, the seas and wilds, the gods: human love is only a small element in the empire of Love/Aphrodite (see on 894).

883. **you range...**: the god is addressed in the second person. Compare 1239-72, though that hymn to Dionysus is a plea to the god to appear; here the god's power is simply asserted by helpless mortals. It is not clear in the line whether fish and animals at pasture are said to be subject to Love or whether there is simply an assertion of Love's influence over the whole earth. Contrast Love's total power with man's doubtful success in taming the physical world (see on 376-416). For Love 'ranging the seas' compare the connection between the sea and passion in this play (see on 661-6); also Eur. *Hippolytus* 443-8 where Aphrodite is said to be irresistible if she comes in a great flood, and to move through the air and in the waves of the sea.

884. The gods were notoriously subject to Love; compare *Women of Trachis* 443 where Love 'rules even the gods as he wishes; *ibid.* 499-502; Eur. fragment 434 'Love attacks not just men, nor indeed women, but also stirs up the lives of gods above.' It is common, incidentally, for mortals in tragedy to excuse their amorousness by recalling the susceptibility of the gods; see e.g. Eur. *Hippolytus* 453ff.

887-8. **you...swerve them to their ruin**: compare 687ff. In that last ode, the over-ambitions were said to be ruined; here even the just are brought low by Love. The chorus is asserting the pessimistic general truth that mortals are subject to a universal force to which human morality is irrelevant (while in the last ode mortals were subject to a divine force which paid great attention to human morality). Humanity is very small in the face of these great forces.

894. **you mock us**: the mockery of Aphrodite marks her effortless superiority. For the ode in general compare Soph. fragment 941 'Children, Cypris (Aphrodite) is called not only Cypris but many names. She is Hades, she is life that wastes not away, she is frenzy and madness, she is invincible desire, she is lamentation. In her all is

activity, all rest, all violence. She melts into all who have the breath of life. What passageway is not open to this goddess? She attacks the swimming race of fish, she is in the four-legged offspring of the land, she flies her wing among the birds...in beasts, in mortals, in the gods above. Which god does she not wrestle with and throw in three falls? If I may say it, and I may speak the truth, she rules the heart of Zeus without spear and without sword. Cypris cuts short, you see, all plans of gods and men.'

895-1034. *Antigone laments the cruel death she faces and the prospects she might have had. Creon remains firm and unrepentant.*

895ff. On the animated rhythms of the following scene see Knox.

900ff. The choral lyric is continued in a long lyrical exchange (*commos*) between Antigone and the chorus, and the *commos*, as often, is a lament. Why does Antigone, hitherto so strong and determined to die (see e.g. note on 86), change her tone in these emotional lyrics? For it is a change of tone, from resolution to regret, not a change of intent. We must, I think, look for dramatic and thematic reasons rather than psychological speculations (though Creon's remark at 654-5 could be right: 'Even the bravest will cut and run, once they see Death coming for their lives').

(i) Tragic heroines who are resolved on death frequently lament the life they are leaving, having elsewhere said that life was worthless; compare note on 512-20, Eur. *Hecuba* 411-18, Eur. *Iphigenia in Aulis* 1218ff.

(ii) Sophocles has taken great care to isolate Antigone. Isolation is a common feature of the Sophoclean hero(ine), seen in Ajax and Philoctetes at its most extreme; in Antigone's case isolation has been carefully engineered. The chorus of Theban elders has supported Creon and failed to register unease at sinister remarks or violent reactions to an almost incredible degree. Early hints of doubts (see on 236-40) disappear at vital moments (no comment at 554, approval at 761-3) while criticism of Antigone is automatic (525-7), and continues into the lament. Sophocles only allows the chorus to express fears for Creon obliquely in choral odes (passages collected in note on 879-94). Ismene means well but is on a different wavelength from Antigone. Haemon is Antigone's great ally in argument and feeling but they never meet. Lastly, and most poignantly, Antigone is not certain that the gods support her (1013-21).

(iii) Antigone after Creon's change of death sentence (870-8) is now facing a living death. She will be neither in this world, to which she is indifferent, nor in the underworld with her dead relatives, but in some awful intermediate state. She dwells on this state at 905, 915ff, 939-42, 958; and the chorus takes it up at 913-4 and 1035ff. See notes on that ode and 939-42.

(iv) Linked to the theme of the living death is Antigone the bride of Death. The connection between death and marriage was first made by Creon (730), and is fully developed here; see 908, 978.

(v) Sophocles is a master of the exciting and dramatic effect; compare note on 788-809.

(vi) This lament draws out in lyrical form the implications of Creon's misguided decision. What earlier was sinsister (see e.g. notes on 543-6, 735ff.) is now presented as a perversion: the living are to be buried and marriage, properly a union for the creation of new life, is to be with death. It is, I think, her unnatural death that best accounts for Antigone's tone here, for she has close regard for the proper ritual at the proper time. On marriage see further on 905-8.

904. death who puts us all to bed: Death and Sleep are often associated. In *Iliad* 16 the body of Sarpedon is wafted away from the battlefield by Sleep and Death (676-83).

905-8. Acheron...: one of the rivers of the Underworld. The perversion of Antigone's fate (see 900ff.) is brought out by the proper wedding rites she will miss and by the notion of marriage to Death (in this case to Acheron 'the lord of the dark waters') which is no marriage at all. A major part of a Greek wedding was a torchlight procession to the bridegroom's home during which marriage hymns were sung. Now we must remember that Antigone has never spoken of marriage before, unless it is she who speaks 645 (see note in Appendix). Do we conclude that she loves Haemon as he evidently loves her (see on 879-94)? It is a question that Sophocles gives us no means of answering. Rather, we should say that the last scene, and particularly the last ode lead us, the audience, to think of sexual love and marriage, and we can look at Antigone in a new light as a nubile girl denied her natural desires and expectations, indeed her natural functions: her fate is a perversion of the natural order. In the context of lament we might compare two epitaphs from later antiquity: 'My parents, my good brother, my husband did not harvest my youthful beauty; only grim Hades' and 'Grievous Hades came and took you swiftly away when he saw your beauty and blameless character.'

911-14. No withering illness...: the chorus acknowledge that the means of death is unusual (disease and battle are the normal means of premature death) and the state of a living death unique; but they imply that Antigone is responsible. 'A law to yourself' recalls Creon's charge of self-will and lawlessness in Antigone (see e.g. 528ff).

915-24. Niobe: the wife of Amphion (see on 1273), presumed to compare her own children with the children of the goddess Leto; Leto's children Apollo and Artemis shot down Niobe's children (see

Knox). The myth of human presumption and divine wrath was treated in the *Niobe* of Sophocles (papyrus fragments recently found in Egypt and probably from *Niobe* cast new light on Sophocles' treatment of the gods: see D. F. Sutton *The Lost Sophocles* 85-8). Zeus took pity on the weeping Niobe and changed her into a rock (there are many stories in Greek myth of humans transformed into birds, animals, trees etc.). There are several points here.

(i) Sophocles almost certainly intends us to think only of the transformation of Niobe; we should not compare the boasting mother with the dangerous behaviour of Antigone.

(ii) Tantalus was a notable criminal in myth, but again there appears to be no significance here in his mention, nor in the fact that Niobe returned to her home town of Sipylus in Asia Minor (the town of which Tantalus was king) before being transformed into the rock wihch was part of nearby Mount Sipylus.

(iii) This is a passage of remarkable poetry, fusing the physical appearance of part of Mt. Sipylus with the mythical origin of its female shape, Niobe; the loneliness of the mountain with Niobe's grief, the snow and rain with her tears; and through all, the gradual transformation from flesh to stone ('walled her round' (919) is misleading: read 'subdued her' which is what the Greek says). The similarity with Antigone is a subtle one: Niobe eventually became totally rock (that is she died) but the process from flesh to stone was slow, hence a 'living death'. Antigone can expect a lingering death, a living death walled up in the cave. The fate of both women is matter for lamentation.

925.**born of gods**: Niobe was the granddaughter of gods. In a fragment of the *Niobe* of Aeschylus her family are called 'the near-kin of the gods, the relatives of Zeus'; and in Soph. *Electra* 150 the chorus sing 'Niobe, I count you as a god.'

930ff. **you mock me**: Antigone presumably feels mocked because the chorus, while sympathetic, do not acknowledge that she is right and therefore do not see the horror of her (unjust) punishment as she does (for her isolation see on 900ff.). The Greeks were sensitive to mocking laughter: in a value-system where superiority and domination were sought after, mockery was a reminder of inferiority from a superior. Compare for example Eur. *Medea* 797: 'It is unbearable to be laughed at by enemies.'

931. **my fathers' gods**: an oath by the gods of one's ancestors, familiar to any Greek, is particularly appropriate to Antigone, the defender of kin and family gods (cf. 545,736).

934ff. **O my city...**: Antigone's apostrophe of local places marks great emotion. For Dirce see on 121.

939-42. strange new tomb...: the tomb is strange and new because it is a tomb for the living. The Greek word translated by 'stranger' is *metoicos*, that is 'one who dwells in a city, but is a citizen of somewhere else, and has few local civic rights'. By this technical term Antigone expresses her insecurity in the world (a familiar theme from earlier scenes) and her peculiar status as a living corpse among the dead. She is in an equivalent of Christian limbo, an unfamiliar and unnatural notion at this time, perhaps analogous to the unburied corpse (see on 26-36).

943-6. You went too far...: the chorus see Antigone as the traditional criminal in poetic terms. For 'daring' see 415. For attacks on the throne/altar of Justice compare Aesch. *Agamemnon* 385-6 'kicking against the great altar of Justice'; Aesch. *Eumenides* 546-9 'Revere the altar of Justice and do not, with an eye to profit, kick it down with godless foot.' The chorus, then, most surprisingly, continue to accept Creon's valuation of Justice despite the ambiguities of the choral odes and the whole movement of the play. See on 900ff.

947-55. grief for father...: Antigone picks up the chorus's question about family troubles. Her tone here (see on 900ff.) is tragic and hopeless, in the manner of the choral ode at 656ff. There is a change of emphasis from her words in the prologue; see on 2.

956-8. brother, doomed in your marriage: on the marriage of Polynices see Knox. 'Your marriage murders mine' is not in the Greek text.

959. reverence: the chorus, again in lyrics, sing literally 'Reverence is in a sense reverence', conceding perhaps that Antigone showed one kind of reverence in burying her brother, but pointing out that there is more to be revered than that: the laws of the state for example.

960-1. attacks on power: the chorus at their most blind. A tyrant's grip on power is irrelevant to religious morality, for which Antigone is about to die.

962. your passion: words very similar to the chorus's criticism of Antigone at 525-7. For the charge of 'blind will' compare the note on 912 'a law to yourself'.

963-9. No one to weep for me: Antigone's final stanza is a culmination of sorrow, her loneliness emphasised by the lack of family to perform funeral rites (Ismene is forgotten). For the string of negatives see on 5-8, for the loss of a wedding song see on 905-8.

969-71. Can't you see?...: Creon's rhetoric is harsh; compare note on 543-6.

977. stranger's rights: see on 939-42 and Knox on 977.

978. O tomb...: Antigone returns to spoken lines for a long and complicated speech. These calmer lines dispel, if it were needed, any suspicion we may have entertained of a change of mind in Antigone in the lament. She sees her family now not as fellow victims of a curse but as friends to be met in death (see next note). The speech starts on a major theme of the lament, Antigone the bride of Death. The tomb as a bridal chamber (rather than 'bridal-bed') will be important in the death scene; see on 1328.

985ff. **cherishing one good hope**: the expectation of meeting dead relatives after death is common. In *Oedipus the King* Oedipus blinds himself partly for a practical reason, so that he will not after death see the family he has polluted (see 1500ff). In Eur. *Alcestis* Admetus says (363-4) 'Expect me there and prepare a house so that you can live with me' to his dying wife. Similar thoughts appear on epitaphs: 'I live with my husband'; 'The sun looked upon us as we lived a life in common; now a single tomb has received our old bodies in death'; 'You lie near your son, your limbs touching; gladly did you leave life to join the one who died before.'

988. **Eteocles** (988) and **as well** (992) are inserted by Fagles (see Knox), I think rightly. There is then a contrast in 'But now' (991) between the members of the family buried in the proper way, and the unhappy Polynices. But some have argued that Eteocles is so little mentioned in the play that we should understand Polynices in 988; *he* is the brother Antigone wishes to lie beside in death (see 87).

989-90. **When you died...**: funeral rites. For the washing of the corpse see 1323, for the poured cups (libations) see 478-80, and note on 220. The rituals of burial are reverently performed alsewhere in Sophocles; see *Ajax* 1403ff., *Oedipus at Colonus* 1810ff. Much of the latter play is a powerful testament to the religious feelings of the poet and his city.

995-1012. **Never, I tell you...**: this passage is surprising in argument, seeming to ignore the great laws Antigone championed at 499ff. in favour of a curious statement on the ease or difficulty of replacing different members of a family, a statement also made in a passage by Sophocles' friend, Herodotus the historian. See the very fine discussion by Knox in the Penguin Introduction, 45-50. As Knox says, Aristotle's support of the passage in the fourth century is persuasive; but it would be a bold person who affirmed that Sophocles *certainly* wrote these lines.

1013-21. **What law of the mighty gods**: Antigone expresses her utter isolation in doubts about the gods (see on 900ff.). She has one comrade, Haemon (for the image compare 827-8 'this boy, I do believe, is fighting on her side, the woman's side'), but Sophocles does not allow them to meet (see on 900ff.). For the paradox 'my reverence only brands me for irreverence' (1016) compare note on 86. The paradox is a bitter reminder of the chorus's words at 959 (see note) which challenged Antigone's claims to reverence.

1022-34. **Still the same rough winds...**: Antigone's final exchange on stage is in animated rhythm. The chorus remain convinced of her dangerous passion to the end; compare note on 526. The metaphor of 'rough winds, the wild passion raging' recalls earlier imagery of storms at sea; see on 661-6. Antigone's last words are of her city (compare 934ff.) and its gods, specifically 'the first gods of the race'. These are not just ancestral gods of the family, i.e. patron gods (compare note on 931), but the progenitors of her family (see genealogy in Knox, p.425) which founded Thebes (Cadmus is the mythical founder). She dies then, defiantly asserting her position in the city and her claims to reverence (compare previous note).

1035-90. *A choral ode in two pairs of lyrical stanzas.*

This is a fascinating ode recalling a number of themes and images in the play, but not easy to interpret precisely. The ode, uniquely in this play (apart from Antigone's comparison of herself with Niobe at 915-24), comments on the action with illustrations from other myths. Just as most tragedies take a myth or part of a myth to shed light on some aspect of life, either the human condition in general or particular preoccupations of the time, or usually both, so within plays, on a smaller scale, other myths are brought in. This is a practice inherited from Homer (see for example *Iliad* 9, *Odyssey* 19.518ff.) and archaic poetry. In this ode, three myths are partly used, Danae (1035-50), Lycurgus (1051-65), and Cleopatra (1066-1090), and it is the partial use of a longer story that introduces problems (see notes below). The principal connections between the ode and its context are imprisonment (Antigone, Danae and Lycurgus are all shut up alive), anger leading to violent words and deeds (Creon, Lycurgus, the new wife of Phineus (1073)), the power of fate (1045, 1088-90, Creon's final scenes), the power of the gods (Dionysus 1054, 1239ff.; Ares 1072; Zeus 1043-4, 677ff.; Aphrodite 879ff.).

1035-50. **Danae**: for the story of Danae see Knox. The suffering of Danae is presented as a consolation for Antigone ('my child, my child, 1042', just as e.g. in *Iliad* 5.382ff. Dione, the mother of the wounded Aphrodite consoles her with a reminder of how Ares, Hera and Hades bore up under their wounds. Like Antigone, Danae is buried alive; the vault is called a tomb; and she is thought of in the context of marriage (for Antigone see on 900ff.). Zeus visited Danae: are the chorus encouraging Antigone to hope for divine intervention? Danae was an innocent sufferer: do the chorus suggest, contrary to their words in the lament, that Antigone suffers unjustly? 1045-50 may lead us to think so, for they speak of the power of fate undermining wealth, armies, ships etc., symbols of the state ruled by Danae's father Acrisius. If Acrisius is subject to fate, then by analogy Creon will be; see Knox. Images of yoking and treasure are not chance reminiscences of Creon's metaphors (see on 331-2 and 335-41): there is perhaps an ironic contrast between the power of Zeus and of Creon.

1051-65. **The yoke tamed him too...**: Lycurgus too is yoked; for the details of his crime and fate see Knox. But the chorus seem to have moved on from consolation, for although Lycurgus was imprisoned like Antigone, and is called mad and frenzied (on Antigone's madness see e.g. on 81 and 1022-34), he was a notorious *theomachos*, a fighter against a god. If anyone is opposing gods in this play it is Creon, and as Knox says there is an analogy with Creon in opposition to women (see on 593) and in unwise taunting (about Zeus 545, 736; about death 876ff.). Creon is also as passionate as Antigone. Lycurgus seems to be a warning to Creon on the subject of imprisonment; also perhaps on the subject of Dionysus, for it could be said that Creon is under the observation of Dionysus, the patron of Thebes, who was invoked in the first choral song (171) and is asked to appear at 1239-72. Shortly after that ode Creon is destroyed. The present stanza emphasises the passion of Lycurgus; but part of his mistake was to curtail the religious passions of the holy women ('raving sacred cries' 1064). This passionate entanglement between man and god bodes ill for Creon, for in this passionate play Antigone has the gods on her side.

1053. **Edonia**: a kingdon of Thrace, a land associated in this play with violence and passion; see next stanza and note on 661-6.

1057. **his terrible flowering rage burst**: literally 'the fierceness and blossoming strength of his madness dripped away'. Metaphors of flowers and water are mixed; compare Appendix on 673-7. The connection of thought is probably this: there is a similarity between the life-blood of a human and the sap of a plant, and in early Greek thought the life-force leaving the body was associated with drying out. The force of madness is seen as analogous to the life force and can be said to dry out, as in Solon's phrase 'good government dries out the growing flowers of delusion'. Sophocles has taken 'drying out' a stage further to 'dripping away'.

1065. **the Muses**: Dionysus and the Muses are closely related: they in some versions nursed him as an infant, and he presided over their sphere of poetry and the arts.

1066ff. The last two stanzas are a little unclear. The king in 1073 is Phineus, his new queen Eidothea or Idaea, and his former wife Cleopatra. Not only are they not named, but Sophocles expects the audience to supply vital information. Or he seems to expect it: as the lines stand it seems difficult to make the connections with our play that were made in previous stanzas. The entire ode is allusive, the first stanza perhaps to Soph. *Acrisius* and *Danae*, the second to Aeschylus' triology on Lycurgus, and the last two to any of three plays Sophocles wrote on the family of Phineus. Knox and Fagles assume that Sophocles intends us to think of imprisonment in these stanzas as in the previous two, and they are supported by the ancient commentator on the passage; see Knox. They may be right, but there is an alternative. If Sophocles wanted imprisonment to be the main point of these two stanzas he would have said so; at best then it must remain in the back of the audience's mind. There is a general movement in the ode away from inprisonment towards violence. Danae is an entombed bride (1039) but Acrisius is neither violent nor angry; Lycurgus is imprisoned for his violent anger; the new queen 'rearing in rage' stabs the princes' eyes (in some detail, 1075-5) and their suffering is described (1077-8), along with cries for revenge. It seems to me clear that we must associate Creon with violence (to Antigone, to the gods, to the natural order) and Antigone with suffering. And the princes' mother (Cleopatra), although of unusual birth (her father was 'the wild North Wind' 1085), is like Antigone in her noble family (her mother Oreithyia was the daughter of an Athenian king (1083); for Antigone's family see on 1022-34) and in her harsh treatment by fate. The main suggestion of the ode seems then to be that Creon and Antigone, hitherto seen as antagonists in questions of morality, are victims of fate (1045, 1088ff.); that Creon is inflicting violence and Antigone suffering it; and that there will be repercussions (1077).

1066. **far north**: the unhappy story of family violence in the house of Phineus takes place in Thrace (compare note on 1053).

1075. **dagger-shuttle**: a shuttle drew the cross-threads through the vertical threads held on the loom in weaving. Eidothea, one of the bad violent women of tragedy (cf. note on 593), uses a woman's implement as her weapon. Compare the blinding of Polymestor in Eur. *Hecuba* where the Trojan women use the brooches from their clothing (1035-1182).

1080-1. Delete these invented lines (see Knox for their presence in the translation).

1085. **North Wind**: Sophocles combines three common aspects of the North Wind (Boreas): he is a literal wind, a stallion (a representation of his speed), and the husband of a princess.

1089. **everlasting Fates**: the contrast between mortals and divine forces which are not subject to time is constantly drawn; compare note on 677-86.

1090-1238. *Tiresias tells Creon the stark facts about his refusal to bury Polynices and his decision to bury Antigone alive. Creon reacts angrily but soon crumbles into submission.*

1090. Enter Tiresias the prophet. Dramatically his appearance in this play differs from *Oedipus the King*. His early appearance there allows time before the climax for Oedipus to argue with him and reject his warnings; here Creon argues but is forced, because matters are critical, to yield. Tiresias' words are authoritative.

1097. **straight on course**: thanks to the teaching of Tiresias Creon has hitherto been a safe helmsman of the state. But the play has shown Creon rejecting all teaching from others (passages collected at note on 1470) and the dangerous associations of the sea (see on 661-6). Creon will only return to a true course when he accepts once more the teaching of Tiresias. See also Knox.

1100. **razor-edge**: for the image compare *Iliad* 10.173-4 'Whether there is gloomy death or life for the Achaeans stands on the razor's edge.'

1101ff. **You will learn...**: in the Greek world prophecy was an art of which the interpretation of the behaviour of birds was a large part. Omens could be seen in their flight, in where they came to rest, in how they fed, and in the sounds they uttered. The mutual destruction of the birds in the sanctuary is a bad but uncertain omen requiring verification by other means (see 1110ff.). For the use of birds in the play see on 471ff.

1104. **sanctuary**: literally 'harbour'. The language of the sea, associated extensively with disorder (see on 661-6), now includes harbours as places not of safety but of disruption. Compare 1413.

1110ff. **I was afraid...**: Tiresias' second method of divination is the inspection of the entrails of animals offered in burnt-sacrifice. In the burning the vigour of the fire (hence 'ignited at all points') and the movement of the flames was significant, and too much smoke or feeble flames a bad sign. The fat wrapped round the thigh bones (1115) ought to have taken light and the organs ought to have remained intact to allow examination of their shape and colour. The failure of the fire and the melting of the fat into a sputtering ooze mark the rejection of the offering by the gods. The bones glistening white and the soft ooze are intended to remind us of the putrifying body of Polynices (453-4): both are displeasing to the gods. See also Knox.

1123. **your high resolve**: Creon's resolve (the Greek word is *phrēn* which has been widely used in the play: it is a word of multiple meaning, depending on context but all relating to emotional and mental states) is impugned by Tiresias. This authoritative statement immediately brings into question all Creon's earlier conduct. By 'plague' Tiresias means religious pollution. For the association between disease and pollution see *Oedipus the King* 1-314. For the associations of disease in the play see 465 ('a black plague of the heavens'), 819 ('isn't that just the sickness that's attacked her?'). In the ode on civilisation, disease is part of the natural order that man tries to control (405); but as with the other parts of nature, the play seems to show that man's control is either illusory or at best ambivalent.

1124. **hearths are fouled**: Creon had thought the non-burial of Polynices was in the city's interest. His failure to consider the gods properly has resulted in the pollution of public and private religion. For Creon's failure even to consider private religion see on 543-6.

1129-30. **No birds cry out...**: total confusion in the religious and natural world. The birds that ought to give omens (see on 1101ff.) are eating fat which ought to burn in sacrifice (see on 1110ff.), and, worse, the fat is human fat, mixed with blood, and dead. The birds of this world are making food of a corpse that should have found honour in the Underworld.

1131-7. **Take these things to heart...**: with traditional advice Tiresias urges Creon to change: in 1135 read 'if he tries to cure himself' (Fagles' 'make amends' obscures a medical image). Tiresias offers a hopeful outcome if Creon recognises his state of mind ('stubborness...stupidity') and in the end it is Creon's stubbornness that seals his fate, for he does not reach Haemon and Antigone in time (compare note on 1318ff).

1138. **yield to the dead**: on yielding in Sophocles see on 788-809. Yielding to the dead ought to be easier in the Greek value-system for the dead are incapable of asserting superiority (compare note on 930ff.).

1146. **fortune-teller**: read 'seer'. While Creon's words are similar to Oedipus' attack on Tiresias at *Oedipus the King* 432ff., Creon does not use words of abuse like quack and fortune-teller that Oedipus uses.

1149. **drive your bargains**: charges of bribery against seers appear in literature (see the speech of Oedipus noted above) and fifth-century history (for an example of alleged bribery at Delphi see Thucydides 5.16); but Creon's string of commercial images recall earlier speeches (see on 335-41) and confirm his refusal to comprehend the religious implications of his policies. For the silver-gold of Sardis see Knox.

1152-3. **eagles rip the corpse**: a gross impiety, if only a rhetorical fantasy. Creon combines his disrespect for Zeus (compare note on 543-6, 736) with further outrages in the world of birds (see on 471ff.

and 1101ff.). Eagles were traditionally Zeus' birds.

1156. we can't defile the gods: an unfortunate trick of words. Although the gods are greater than anything mortals can do to them, they are permanently sensitive to defilement of any kind.

1157-61. No, reverend old Tiresias...: ironic lines. It is Creon who believes he knows what wisdom is (and does not), whose words and actions are obscene to the gods, and who deludes himself with rhetoric. He does not act for gain, but his mind is constricted by seeing gain as the main motive in any who oppose him (see on 335-41).

1162-80. A sequence of stichomythia heightens the tension (see on 568-649) and continues the themes of mental state (cf. note on 1131-7), illness (see on 1123) and profiteering (see on 1149).

1181. learn this by heart!: Tiresias is stung into spelling out the truth brutally, just as he does in *Oedipus the King* 464ff.

1184. your own flesh and blood: Antigone's claims for kinship were supported earlier in the play by reference to shared blood and a shared womb (see especially on 1); and Creon did not challenge this association (see 735f. 'let her cry...to Zeus who defends all bonds of kindred blood'). Now that Creon's neglect of kinship is to be punished by the loss of his closest family, similar bodily terms reinforce the loss.

1185-93. a corpse for corpses...: Tiresias spells out in religious terms the confusion Creon has brought to the natural order of things: the living (Antigone) is buried and the dead (Polynices) unburied, an affront to the gods of the upper world and the gods of the Underworld (in this schematic arrangement we should not worry that Zeus is a god with power in both worlds; compare note on 499-510). Tiresias' words, though only a prediction, are soon proved true, and Haemon and Antigone become corpses with Polynices. The deaths of Haemon and Antigone, as described by the messenger (1312ff.), are comprehensible in human terms of despair and grief, but the religious meaning Tiresias puts on these deaths is most important. The death of Haemon is the price Creon must pay for entombing Antigone and not burying Polynices ('a corpse for corpses given in return'); the rule of the gods, under which sinners must pay, has superseded the rule of Creon, and the king is now held to account for those earlier incidents where we felt unease (see especially on 463ff., 499ff., 870-8, 900ff.) but could not be sure because of ambiguities in the conduct of Antigone, Haemon and the chorus. See also Knox's note.

1194-7. the avengers: the instruments of the gods' punishment are the Furies, associated in particular with the dead and the gods of the Underworld, but also with Zeus and the Olympians. The notion of the

Furies coming slowly but surely ('late but true to the mark') is probably another reminiscence of Aeschylus (see notes on 656-700); compare for example Aesch. *Agamemnon* 62-5, Aesch. *Libation Bearers* 379-82. The idea is traditional however. For the Furies lying in wait for a victim compare Soph. *Electra* 490 'the bronze-footed Fury lurking in her terrible ambush'.

1200. **mourning cries for men and women**: Knox and Fagles see an allusion to the deaths of Haemon and Eurydice, but the Greek could mean 'mourning cries of men and women', that is, general lamentation.

1201-5. **Great hatred**: now that the tables have been turned on Creon (see on 1185-93) he faces the consequences not only of his failure to bury Polynices but also of his neglect of the bodies of Polynices' comrades. These are the Argives and their leaders referred to (obscurely) at 12-13 and in the first choral ode. See Knox. The hatred Tiresias mentions gave rise to an attack on Thebes by the sons of the Argives, an attack which Sophocles portrayed in his famous *Epigonoi (The After-born)*, for which see Sutton *The Lost Sophocles* 37-42. Many scholars are uneasy about this belated reference to the unburied Argives and doubt if Sophocles wrote these lines.

1208. **arrows deadly true**: the image of arrows for strong words or passions is common in poetry; compare 1145.

1216. **Since the hair on this old head...**: the chorus-leader means 'I am an old man and have never found Tiresias to be wrong.'

1218. **I'm shaken**: Creon listens to advice for the first time and at 1223 is willing to obey. It is rare for a Sophoclean hero to yield a point or change his/her mind (see on 788-809), though it is possible, even likely, that there are cases in some of the lost plays. Creon's decision to yield is the most striking of all (Neoptolemus' change of mind in Philoctetes amounts to a return to normal conduct), and it is for the audience to decide whether a belated recognition of the wishes of the gods is the mark of a tragic hero or of a weak lesser figure. Creon must be judged beside Antigone in this respect, for she conforms to the norm in Sophocles. Note that Creon approaches his change of mind in a state of shock (1218, literally 'troubled in my mind') and acknowledges his spirit, his 'pride'. He now admits what the audience has long realised, that his state of mind is of the greatest significance in his actions; compare e.g. note on 845-6. See also 1229.

1227-8. **Disasters sent by the gods**: literally described as 'swift of foot'. The agents of the gods' swift punishment are often personified in this way; compare *Iliad* 9.505-7 'Infatuation the strong and swift-footed because she far outstrips the others and is first to harm men in all lands'.

1237. **the established laws**: a further stage in Creon's admission of error: hitherto he has seen law only in terms of his edict, but the established laws include the traditions of a city and the laws of the gods.

1239-72. *A choral ode in two pairs of lyrical stanzas in the form of a hymn to Dionysus.*

The hymn is in the usual Greek pattern of a call upon the god by name (1239), a list of his holy places and attributes (1240-60), prayer ('come' 1261) with reasons (1261-3). The hymn is built up over the first three stanzas leading to the appeal 'come' in 1261, with the final stanza repeating the appeal and one of the god's holy names, Iacchus, in 1271. The hymn is inspired first of all by Tiresias' statement about a plague in Thebes (1123); the city's god (1240, 1245, 1259) is urged to come with his 'healing stride' (1263), just as in *Oedipus the King* the first choral ode (169-244) is an appeal to the city's gods, and especially Apollo the Healer, to bring an end to plague and death. But the hymn is also joyful and hopeful; now that Creon has bowed to the will of the gods the chorus believe that danger will be averted. For the audience, however, there are two ominous considerations.

(i) On a formal level Sophocles writes a joyful ode to the gods in other plays just before disaster strikes (compare *Ajax* 693-718, *Oedipus the King* 1195-1214); it is part of his dramatic technique to offer the excitement of hopes raised only to be dashed the next moment (compare note on 788-809).

(ii) Dionysus has ambiguous associations in the play. He was called upon to lead the city to peace in the first ode (171); but one of his manifestations is ecstasy or religious madness (1064, 1246, 1256), and we can at least wonder how such a god will bring Creon to safety given the prominence in the play of madness and folly. When Lycurgus uttered mad taunts against Dionysus his punishment was severe (see further on 1051-65). Note too that the violent Capaneus is brought low after being 'mad for attack, ecstatic' (147-51): the Greek for 'ecstatic' (*baccheuon*) means literally 'possessed by Bacchus/Dionysus'. See also Knox.

1239. **God of a hundred names!**: many Greek gods had different titles, depending upon cult and location, but Dionysus had more than most. In this ode his name Bacchus comes from Lydia in Asia Minor, and Iacchus, a god of the Eleusinian mysteries, was identified with Dionysus by the fifth century.

1240-1. **Semele**: Dionysus was the son of the mortal Semele and Zeus; the god came in his full force as god of thunder and lightning and killed her, but protected the unborn Dionysus in his thigh. Euripides rationalised this story, and the supposed multiple origin of Dionysus (in Asia and Thrace as well as Thebes) in his *Bacchae*.

1242. **the famous lands of evening**: literally 'Italy', a reference to the worship of Dionysus in the Greek cities of Southern Italy, showing the extent of the god's powers.

1243-54. For the place names see Knox. The hills of Eleusis are said to 'welcome in the world' because the Mysteries were a cult for all cities, not for Eleusis alone. For Ismenus see on 121, for the field sown with the Dragon's teeth see Knox on 117-79. Thebes is called the mother-city of the frenzied women (literally 'of the Bacchae') because the rites of Dionysus were first celebrated in Greece at Thebes. See the *Bacchae* of Euripides.

1249-53. **we have seen you...**: Dionysiac rites were celebrated near Delphi, the seat of the oracle of Apollo, principally on the hills above the city. Every other year local women held a torch-light festival in the uplands between the mountain peaks and were driven mad by the god in a way similar to that protrayed by Euripides in the *Bacchae*. Euripides explicitly mentions this festival at Delphi at *Bacchae* 306ff.

1254-5. **ivy...vines**: the ivy and the vine are the plants principally associated with Dionysus.

1261-72. **come, Dionysus!**: Dionysus is asked first to come (1261) and then to 'come forth' (literally 'appear', 'reveal yourself'). He is visualised both in anthropomorphic terms as one who strides down mountain sides as a healer, and as lord of the dancing, and also as a power in the universe who causes the stars to dance and mortals to lose their senses. The sacred dances of Dionysus generally took place at night (see 170, 1249-53), but such ritual was not exclusive to Dionysus; Athena for example was similarly honoured in Athens.

1272-1470. *The final scene* (exodos) *in which the deaths of Haemon, Antigone and Eurydice are announced and Creon comes to terms with his punishment.*

1271ff. The messenger speech is a major feature in Greek tragedy which broadly serves two purposes. The first is practical: violence was not admitted to the stage (though there are exceptions: in Sophocles *Ajax* the hero may have killed himself on stage, and in *Niobe* Artemis may have been shown shooting Niobe's children (see reference in note on 915-24)); consequently the violent parts of the myths used in tragedy were reported in a long narrative. The second is artistic: here was an opportunity for sustained and detailed narrative that otherwise was more suitable to epic than drama. Sophocles used his messenger speeches to great effect, most notably in *Electra* where the report of

Orestes' death in a chariot race, for all its detail, is false, and part of the deception of Clytemnestra. In general the messenger gives a detached and factual account with a minimum of his own comment, apart from general reflections on the lessons to be learnt, as here. The messenger speech proper begins at 1312.

1273. **Cadmus and the kings**: literally 'Cadmus and Amphion'. For Cadmus see Knox on 117-79. Amphion was the husband of Niobe (see on 915-24) and a lyre-player who with his music caused stones magically to build themselves into a city wall for Thebes.

1271-7. **there's not a thing...settled**: the sentiment is similar to the chorus's words at 677ff. (see on 677-86). For the mutability of human affairs compare *Women of Trachis* 126f. 'the son of Cronos, the ruler of all has not imposed a painless lot on mortals, but sorrow and joy come circling round to all, like the turning paths of the Great Bear.'

1285ff. **squandered his true joys...**: for the thought compare Simonides (lyric poet early fifth century) fragment 71 'Without joy what human life is to be desired or what kingly power? Without it not even the gods' existence is enviable.'

1286. **a living corpse**: Creon's lot is likened to the living death whose prospect Antigone found so awful (see on 900ff.). But the metaphor is common in the present context; compare *Philoctetes* 1018 'friendless, deserted, without a city, a corpse among the living'.

1290. **a wisp of smoke**: literally 'a shadow of smoke'. The frailty of humanity or of human happiness is elsewhere compared with a shadow, often in combination with some other insubstantial thing; compare Aeschylus fragment 399 'human thought is ephemeral and nothing is to be believed any more than a shadow of smoke.'

1300. Enter Eurydice. She speaks only nine lines, listens to the messenger speech and leaves. Her dramatic function is to make visible the family Creon has neglected in the play and which now destroys itself in suicide.

1305. **queen Athena**: the Thebans appeal to Athena for help in *Oedipus the King*, at 25 and 180-1.

1312-17. **I'll speak as an eye-witness...**: messengers regularly support their story by stressing that it is an eye-witness report; similarly they consider the effect on their listeners. The sentry earlier in the play gives an exaggerated form of this convention.

1318ff. Creon buries Polynices first and then goes to Antigone's prison. Some critics have seen an element of bad luck in this order of priorities: would Antigone and Haemon have been reached in time if Polynices had been left until later?

1319. **the edge of the plain**: it is reasonably clear that Sophocles (or his predecessors) envisaged Polynices' body lying to the north of the city where the plain meets higher ground (see 1233 and note on 455). The area contained rocky caves where Antigone's prison could be made.

1321. On Hecate of the Crossroads, see Knox.

1323. **a bath of holy water**: in normal circumstances the corpse was washed in water heated in a cauldron and annointed with unguents; compare the burial of Ajax at *Ajax* 1402ff.

1328. For Antigone the 'bride of Death' see on 905-8. As the messenger's story unfolds we see Haemon and Antigone, the perfect couple (cf. 643 'never as true, as close a bond as theirs), united not in marriage but in death; see 1330-1, 1349-50, 1352, 1365-71. Creon's policy which brought disruption to the natural order of things is now seen at its most tragic.

1333. **the strange...cry**: Antigone uttered the cries of a bird when she saw the body of Polynices again dishonoured (471); Tiresias' birds uttered a strange unintelligible voice (1106); Creon is now punished with the 'strange inscrutable cry' of his own son.

1358-9. **a wild burning glance**: Haemon's response to his anxious father is a wild glance and speechlessness. We are bound to recall Creon's earlier language of taming wild animals (see on 331-2) and the confidence of the second ode in describing man's achievements in taming wild animals and being able to speak (which animals do not do); compare note on 376-416. With the utmost irony Creon's policy of 'taming' the city has reduced his own son to bestiality.

1359. **spat in his face**: for spitting as a sign of loathing compare Aeschylus *Prometheus* 1070 'There is no disease I spit out more than this (i.e. treachery).'

1362. **desperate with himself**: Creon has recogised the error of his policy, but he is unable to control the passions of those he loves. Haemon is 'raging mad' (1297), insane and mad (1356).

1365-71. In death Haemon and Antigone lie together like bride and groom (for the details see Knox on 1346-7), an ironic but literal consummation of the bride of death imagery of the lament (see on 905-8). In the Greek in 1372 Haemon is the subject of 'shows' not Creon.

1374f. **The lady's gone...**: women leave the Sophoclean stage in silence at *Women of Trachis* 813ff., *Oedipus the King* 1179ff.; the silent exit leads to suicide.

1388ff. **The king himself**: with the death of Haemon the chorus now fully accept Creon's folly (contrast e.g. 525-7, and note on 861), and their judgment of his 'madness' and 'blind wrongs' is picked up by Creon himself in his lament (1393, 1394, 1397, 1400 etc.). The chorus chant in animated rhythm in anticipation of Creon's lament.

1392-1470. Creon's lament, concluded by five lines of chanted rhythm from the chorus. With the exception of three lines (1410, 1438, 1456) Creon sings in lyrical stanzas which are offset by the calm spoken lines of the chorus and messenger. As with Antigone's lament (commos), Creon's distressed lyrics mark his isolation. The chorus emphasise that the guilt is wholly his own, no longer considering the conduct of Antigone or Haemon (1391 'proof of his own madness, no one else's') or any harshness in the fate he has suffered. This should alert us to the use of the chorus earlier: their dogged loyalty to Creon against Antigone and Haemon is sufficient at face value, but also has the dramatic function, particularly in Antigone's case, of leaving them alone, and arousing in the audience admiration and fear for their conduct (compare note on 900ff.).

1400-1. **too late**: Creon learns too late what justice means; compare the words of Dionysus in Eur. *Bacchae* after he has punished the family of Cadmus (1345): 'You recognised me too late, and when you should have recognised me you did not know me.' For learning in general see on 1470.

1403. **the god came down**: for the image of the avenging god as a great force leaping on, or trampling the victim compare 1465; Aeschylus *Persians* 515-6 'O intractable god who leap on the whole Persian race with your tremendous weight'; Aeschylus *Agamemnon* 1176 'some malign god of great weight falling upon you'; *ibid* 1694 'struck by the heavy hoof of the god'; Soph. *Oedipus the King* 300 'fate swooped at his head'.

1404. **wild savage path**: Creon acknowledges his savagery, just as he was confronted with Haemon as a savage. For the irony see on 1358-9.

1411. **mother to the end**: literally 'all-mother', mother in every respect. At Aeschylus *Prometheus* 90 the earth is described as 'all-mother'. The word underlines the extent of the damage brought by Creon on the family.

1413. **harbor of Death**: for the nautical image compare note on 1104. While Hades as the harbour of all the dead was an idea familiar to the Greeks, we should think specifically of the dead from the house of Oedipus where one death demands another (see on 666-77).

Cleansing (*catharsis*) in Greek thought had a religious dimension (purification, cleansing from guilt) and a medical one (purging dangerous vapours in the body). Creon is thinking principally in religious terms: the gods do not allow purification for the treatment of the body of Polynices, but demand in atonement Haemon and now Eurydice. In terms of the imagery of disease, the gods do not allow purgation for the plague Creon has brought on the city (see on 1123):

we may detect another ironic reflection on the civilisation ode (376-416), for disease was one of the aspects of nature man appeared to have conquered.

1426. **she stabbed herself at the altar**: ironically, the altar is probably that of Zeus of the Courtyard of whom Creon spoke slightingly at 545.

1428-9. **Megareus**: one of the defenders of Thebes against the Argive attack; see Aesch. *Seven against Thebes* 473ff. and Knox's note on 1096. Fagles is wrong to add to the Greek text 'killed in the first assault', for Euripides gives him a more spectacular death (and the name Menoeceus) at *Phoenician Women* 911ff. and it is impossible to say which version Sophocles has in mind.

1453-8. **That will come when it comes...**: after all the actions and passions of the play order is restored, and human aspiration which in the civilisation ode looked unstoppable is once more subject to the gods (1455) and fate (1458; for 'the doom we must endure' read 'the doom that is destined').

1466-70. **Wisdom**: the play ends as often with a short moral reflection. Wisdom, i.e. right-thinking, has been a major theme of the play, or at least the subversion of wisdom by various states of mind. Tiresias showed that Antigone, for all her fiery conduct, thought aright, because she revered the gods, and that Creon did not because he neglected them. 'The mighty words of the proud' clearly refer to Creon, and ironically recall the first choral ode (140 'Zeus hates with a vengeance all bravado') which described Creon's enemies. The lesson in wisdom which Creon has had to learn has been a hard one.

1470. **teach us wisdom**: learning and teaching have been a major theme of the play, and Sophocles sets up Creon as a teacher of his subjects. At 194 he says 'you cannot know (literally 'learn thoroughly about') a man completely...'; 353 'you'll have learned at last...'; 795-814 Haemon urges Creon to learn but is sharply rebuked; 877 'she may learn at last'. Creon's role as teacher is part of his control over subordinates, but in the event it is he who has to learn, and when his 'teaching' is exposed by Tiresias ('I will teach you' says Tiresias at 1095) his control crumbles (1218ff. and note). But Sophocles as poet and dramatist is also a teacher (tragic poets in their capacity as producers of their own plays were called teachers, and the term implies more than drilling actors and chorus in their parts), and the audience, in addition to witnessing the hard lesson that Creon learns, are shown in the choral odes both traditional wisdom (see e.g. on 140-1, 656-700), and some of the most modern thought (e.g. note on 376-416). The teaching of those odes is woven so deeply into the ironies and subtleties of the play that the audience leaves the theatre not with a 'moral' or a 'message' but a lesson as complex as life itself.

Appendix

The Greek text is disputed in a number of places. A selection of passages relevant to this commentary is given below.

409. weaves in: treat this phrase with extreme caution (see Knox). I think it likely that Sophocles wrote 'when he honours...'.

645-9. There is considerable doubt over who speaks 645, 647, 649; see Knox. Many critics have thought that Antigone speaks 645, but in the circumstances it is impossible to insist that she speaks this one affectionate line to Haemon, still less to base any interpretation upon it. See further on 900ff.

673-77. If the text is sound (which is far from certain) the light 'springing up from' (but literally 'above') the last root is said to be 'cut down' (literally 'mown down') by the 'bloody knife', 'a senseless word', 'fury at the heart'. By the last root Sophocles means Antigone (and Ismene?). Fagles attempts to ease the mixed metaphor by stressing the idea of hope implicit in light. The manuscripts read not 'bloody knife' but 'bloody dust', thereby compounding the mixed metaphor (see Knox). The problems can be reduced to four: (i) bloody dust or bloody knife?; (ii) do we believe Sophocles mixed his metaphors to this extent?; (iii) is the cutting done by three agents (knife, word and fury), or only by the knife, whose meaning is made clear by 'word' and 'fury'?; (iv) why do the gods of death cut the root (Antigone) when she supports their powers so passionately?

The following opinions are extremely subjective. (i) Read 'bloody dust', and translate 676 as '...by the bloody dust due to the gods of death'. The bloody dust is the dust sprinkled on the corpse of Polynices (a corpse bloodied in the duel with Eteocles) in token burial. I reject 'knife' (a) because the word (*kopis*) denotes a special sort of knife used by butchers and foreign soldiers and is too unusual to be used in the context of the gods of death without further comment, and (b) because it makes the fourth problem easier (see below). (ii) Sophocles mixes metaphor (less violently) elsewhere (see on 1057). (iii) Dust, word and fury all cut down the root. Antigone is to die because she sprinkled the dust on Polynices, spoke to Creon in a way bound to antagonise him (see 528ff. and especially 536-40), and because she suffers from the psychological defects inherited from her father (see on 526). (iv) If we keep Fagles' text we can say that the gods of death cutting down Antigone is not a bad thing but the

69

very thing Antigone has always wanted. There is nothing she values in this world; see on 86. If we read 'bloody dust' with the manuscripts the problem disappears, though the note on 86 is still relevant.

880. laying waste the rich!: most editors believe the Greek text to be extremely dubious.

892. side-by-side with the mighty laws!: most scholars suspect this line. In the Greek text 'throned in power' must go with 891, not with Aphrodite in 893, and it seems unlikely that Sophocles linked the amoral power of Love with the mighty (and just) laws of Zeus of which Antigone spoke at 499ff.

943-6. I am reasonably certain that the notion of supplication (see Knox) is wrong. The principal point is that the idea of *kicking* the throne of justice is expected in this context (see main commentary). 'Smashing' is therefore under suspicion. Some editors believe that the law of the land is meant by justice here, but this is extremely doubtful: understand Justice personified, the sense of right enforced by the gods.

1242. lands of evening: I share the doubts of many critics about the suitability of a mention of Southern Italy between Thebes (1240), Eleusis (1243), Thebes (1245f.), Delphi (1249ff.), Nysa on Euboea (1254), and Thebes (1258), all places in or close to Central Greece. If Sophocles wanted to show the geographical extent of the worship of Dionysus it is odd that he chose only Southern Italy. 'Italy' is probably a corruption of some place-name in Greece.

Select Index and Glossary

(References are to the notes)

Aeschylus (influence of) 140ff, 180, 656-700, 666-77, 1194-7
ambition 406-16, 677-86
Aphrodite 879-94, 894
atē (ruin) 700
birds 125ff., 471ff., Introduction section 8
burial 26-36, (lament) 35, (libations) 220, (washing) 1323, (token dust) 277-80, (of traitors) 222ff.
character, Introduction section 3, (announcement of) 173-9
chorus 117-72, 236-40, 376-416, 656-700, 879-94, 1035-90, 1239-72, 1392-1470
curse (family curse) 2, 656-700
the dead 2, 86, 586-9, 985ff.
death 870-8, (living death) 900ff., 939-42, 1035-90, 1286
Dionysus 1239-72
dramatic technique (excitement) 788-809, 900ff., 1239-72, (mystery) 281ff., 463ff.
fate 264-5, 1066ff., 1453-8
family (see *philia*)
gods 415, 463ff. 499ff. 931, 1066ff.
imagery (and association of ideas) Introduction section 8, 1057, (nature subdued) 331-2, 376-416, 378-85, 593, 642, 1035-50, 1358-9, (money) 335-41, 1149, (military) 741-5, (disease) 1123, 1413, (sea) 180, 661-6, 1104
isolation 900ff. 1392-1470
kinship (see *philia*)
lament (*commos*) 900ff., 1392-1470
laws (unwritten) 499ff., 505, (of gods) 505-8, 686-700, Introduction section 6
learning 1470
madness (see states of mind)
marriage 648, 705-878, (and death) 905-8, 978ff., 1328, 1365-71
messenger-speech 1272ff.
myth (use of) 1035-90, Introduction section 2
nature (perversion of) 900ff., 905-8, 1129-30, 1185-93
philia (kinship/family affection) 1, (policical alliance) 213, (in Athenian society) 1, 543-6
phrēn (heart, mind) 1123, related to *phronein* (to be of sound mind, be wise) 1466-70; for both terms see states of mind
pollution 1123, 1413

prophecy and seers 1090, 1101ff., 1110ff., 1149
sexual love 879-94, 884
state (and invididual) 203-4, 410-6, (and ruler) 328-35, 821-7, (and social fabric) 543-6
states of mind Introduction section 4; 81, 149-51, 314-27, 410-6, 376-416, 510, 526, 686-700, 707-8, 845-6, 879-94, 1051-65, 1123, 1388ff.
stichomythia (one-line exchanges) 568-649, 821-7
thought (modern) 376-416, (traditional) 140-1, 376-416, 406-16, 656-700, 686-700, 1194-7, 1274-7, 1290
Time 677-86, (eternity) 86, 505
value-system (aggressive in Greece) 837-8, 930ff.
women 74-7, 376-7, 593
yielding (in Sophocles) 788-809, 1218
Zeus 677-86, (of the Courtyard) 543-6, (of kinsmen) 735ff., (of the dead) 499-501

Oedipus the King

Introduction to Oedipus the King

1. GREEK TREATMENTS OF THE OEDIPUS STORY

Greek tragedies are normally based on traditional myths, the outlines of which would be familiar to the audience and would be followed by the poet, who, however, had considerable freedom in his treatment of the original story (cf. Aristotle *Poetics* ch.14). Thus we have three versions of the return of Orestes: Aeschylus' *Choephoroi* (Libation-Bearers), Sophocles' *Electra* and Euripides' *Electra*, all retaining the essential element, the killing of Aegisthus and Clytemnestra, but with major differences in treatment, emphasis and detail. Similarly all three poets wrote an *Oedipus*, though the earlier play by Aeschylus and the undatable play by Euripides are lost.

The main sources from which the tragic poets drew their plots were the Homeric poems, other epics (now lost) and the poems of Hesiod; and it should be noted that already in these early poems there were differences of detail in the myths. Homer's *Iliad* mentions Polynices' attack on Thebes (the story of Aeschylus' *Seven Against Thebes*) and also refers to funeral games for the 'fallen' Oedipus (suggesting he had met a violent death). In *Odyssey* 11.271-80 Odysseus meets Oedipus' dead mother, here called Epicaste:

> 'And I saw the mother of Oedipodes, beautiful Epicaste, who wrought a dread deed in the ignorance of her heart, in that she married her own son. And he had killed his own father and married her. And immediately the gods revealed it all to men. But he stayed on in lovely Thebes, enduring sorrows, ruling the Cadmeians, thanks to the deadly counsels of the gods. But she went to the house of Hades, mighty doorkeeper, after that she had fastened a noose on high from the lofty roof, being beset by her sorrow...But to him thereafter she left many sorrows, all those that a mother's Furies accomplish.

(Note the immediate revelation of the truth, Oedipus' continued rule and the absence of any mention of the Sphinx, children, Oedipus' blinding of himself or exile.)

Hesiod mentions fighting 'at seven-gated Thebes for the flocks of Oedipus' and 'the destructive Phix, ruin to Cadmus' folk'. Lost epics also deal with the myth. The *Oedipodeia* ascribed Oedipus' four children to a second wife, while a fragment of the *Thebaid* includes Oedipus' curse on his sons.

Aeschylus won first prize with his Theban Trilogy in 467 B.C.; this was perhaps about 40 years before *O.T.*, so that a few very old men in the audience might have seen it, but most would have heard about it from their fathers. The plays were *Laius* (lost), *Oedipus* (lost) and *Seven Against Thebes*; the lighter satyric drama which followed to make up the tetralogy was the *Sphinx* (lost). Only two words of the *Laius* survive, but one suggests Oedipus was exposed in an earthen pot. The one surviving fragment of Aeschylus' *Oedipus* tells how 'We were coming to the crossroads where three carriage tracks meet at Potniae'. (Potniae is in Boeotia south of Thebes, but Sophocles changed the location to near Daulia in Phocis, west of Thebes, and between Thebes and Delphi.) Is it a survivor speaking or is it Oedipus? *Seven Against Thebes* 772ff. gives a clue to the contents of Aeschylus' *Oedipus* when the chorus refer to the universal honour in which Oedipus was held for 'removing the man-snatching doom from the land', and to his self-blinding and his immediate curse on his sons that they should divide up his property with the sword; this immediate curse is absent from *O.T.*, and in the later *O.C.* at 469ff. Oedipus only curses his sons on the day of his death. One basic difference between the three plays of Sophocles, *Ant., O.T.,* and *O.C.*, written over a period of about forty years, and the three plays of the *Theban Trilogy* is the Aeschylean emphasis on the working of a hereditary curse over three generations of the family.

One of the few fragments of Euripides' *Oedipus* says 'We blinded Oedipus' and a late commentator says that Laius' attendants were the speakers. Interestingly enough, we have another play of Euripides, *the Phoenissae*, produced about 409 B.C., which agrees with Aeschylus and Sophocles in making Oedipus blind himself. This play deals with a later stage in the myth, the last hours of Eteocles and Polynices, the events covered in Aeschylus' *Seven Against Thebes*, but differs from *O.T.* and *O.C.* by having Jocasta still alive and Oedipus locked up in the palace by his sons but going on to survive them. The play had opened with Jocasta reminiscing and giving a potted version of past events broadly similar to the plot of *O.T.*, but having Theban and Corinthian herdsmen (i.e. more than one) involved with the infant Oedipus and a slightly different account of the encounter with Laius.

So we see Euripides having different versions of the myth in two plays. Indeed part of the interest for the audience in a play like *O.T.* would have been in seeing how Sophocles treated the myth.

2. LATER DRAMATISATIONS OF THE *O.T.* THEME

Seneca, the Roman philosopher, politician and tutor of Nero, wrote an *Oedipus* (translated by E.F. Watling for the Penguin Classics: Seneca, *Four Tragedies and Octavia*, pp.205-51). The plot is based on *O.T.* but, unlike Sophocles, has Oedipus accused not by Tiresias but by the ghost of Laius, the magical raising of which is narrated in excessive detail by Creon, and has Jocasta commit suicide on stage - if the play ever was produced. Later plays on the Oedipus theme are by Corneille in 1657, Dryden in 1679 and Voltaire in 1718, all of which differ from *O.T.* by incorporating a subsidiary love plot.

In this century the French stage has seen an *Oedipe* by Gide (1932), *La Machine Infernale* (1934) by Cocteau, who had already written the Latin libretto for Stravinsky's magnificent *Oedipus Rex*, and Ghéon's *Oedipe* (1942).

For details and comments on the twentieth century dramatists see Leo Aylen, *Greek Tragedy and the Modern World* (Methuen 1964), and on the earlier plays the Introduction to Jebb's major edition of *O.T.*

3. ARISTOTLE'S *POETICS* AND *O.T.*

Aristotle's *Poetics* are of general interest for their content and their influence on dramatists, particularly French ones, after their rediscovery in the Renaissance, and of special interest to students of *O.T.* because of the many complimentary references to it. Aristotle (384-322) probably wrote his *Poetics* after he had founded his philosophical school, the Lyceum, at Athens in 335 B.C. The work, therefore, dates to fully two generations *after* the deaths of Euripides and Sophocles. What he does in the *Poetics* is to make generalisations about tragedy based on the common features of those plays which he regards as the best. Much of the *Poetics* is dull and technical, but students of *O.T.* and of drama generally should find ch. 6-8, 10-15 and 18 well worth reading. I add a few observations of particular relevance to *O.T.*

To Aristotle plot is the most important component of tragedy. There should be unity of plot, with each incident following naturally or inevitably from what precedes; though he does not mention *O.T.* here, he is clearly thinking of it. (Aristotle only has one and a half Unities, not three; on Unity of Time see note on 499; he does not even mention Unity of Place.) There should be nothing illogical in the plot; illogicalities in *Oedipus* (Aristotle's and the proper name for *O.T.*) are condoned as being 'outside the tragedy' (15.10, 24.20; see note on 149).

The best plot is 'complex', i.e. it includes *peripeteia* (reversal of the trend of the action) and/or *anagnōrisis* (recognition of the truth). The coming of the Corinthian messenger is given as an example of *peripeteia* at 11.2; best plots are when *peripeteia* and recognition coincide, as in O.T. (*Poetics* 11.5-6). The best recognition arises out of the actual incidents (16.11).

Part of the definition of tragedy in ch.6 reads 'by means of pity and fear effecting a *katharsis*' (a purgation, a removal of harmful excess, a medical term here used by a doctor's son) 'of these emotions'. Aristotle goes on to say that we feel pity for one who suffers misfortune undeservedly and fear for someone like ourselves. In 14.2 he praises *O.T.* for producing pity and fear not out of visual effects but out of the actual events. In 14.13 he suggests Sophocles' character of Oedipus elicits fear and pity well by doing the terrible deed in ignorance and only later recognising the close family relationship.

Character is the second most important component of tragedy. The tragic figure (13.5-7: though Aristotle uses the singular he talks in general terms and avoids any word suggesting 'hero') is the sort of man who is not outstandingly virtuous or just and falls into misfortune not through vice or depravity but through a *hamartia* ('a mistake' or 'a mistaken action perhaps committed in ignorance', rather than 'a flaw of character'); he will be one of those enjoying great glory and good fortune, e.g. Oedipus, Thyestes and distinguished men of such families. Aristotle later adds that the *hamartia* should be a serious one on the part of the kind of man he has described or of someone better rather than worse. The best tragedies are composed about a few houses involving Alcmeon, Oedipus and others who have suffered or done terrible things.

In ch.15 Aristotle says characters should be good, appropriate, true to real life and consistent. He also quotes Sophocles as saying his characters are idealised whereas Euripides depicts men as they are (25.11).

Finally in 26.12 he says tragedy is more effective than epic because it is more concentrated. What would happen if *O.T.* were to be extended to the length of the *Iliad*? All this seems to show that to Aristotle *O.T.* typified the best tragic plot and Sophocles' Oedipus the best tragic characterisation and, therefore, that Sophocles was the best tragic poet.

Notes to O.T.

1-168. *The Prologue: Oedipus listens to the appeals of the children and priest and promises help against the plague. Creon arrives from Delphi with Apollo's message that Laius' killer(s) must be banished.*

The lines of the prologue will be spoken by the actors in the formal metre of tragic dialogue, the six-foot iambic line, see General Introduction section 4. Oedipus' high station will immediately be obvious from his magnificent costume which probably reached to the ground. As Oedipus remains on stage virtually throughout every dialogue scene, (see on 245) his part will be played by one actor, the protagonist.

1. **my children**: the suppliants include priests of various ages and young men and children (see 17-22) but Oedipus as ruler takes a paternal interest in them all.

2. **my altar**: not sacred to Oedipus, but used by him in worship; Oedipus is not on a par with the gods, cf. 39-40. In fact there are several altars of the gods in front of the palace, as we learn from 18.

3. **wound in wool**: see Knox

5. **the Healer**: see Knox.

6-7. Oedipus at once gives the impression of energy, efficiency and an enquiring mind, as well as personal involvement.

8-9. **you all know me...**: this would not have sounded as conceited to a Greek audience as it does to us. Odysseus introduces himself similarly at *Odyssey* 9.19. The Greeks disliked false modesty.

9. **I am Oedipus**: the name means Swollen-Foot.

The audience will appreciate the irony in Oedipus' reference to his fame. He thinks of himself as famous for solving the riddle of the Sphinx; they will think rather, of his 'fame' as the man who killed his father and married his mother.

13-15. These lines add to the favourable impression of Oedipus, by suggesting he is kindly and devoted to the welfare of his subjects.

24. **the squares**: the *agorai* or market-places, of which ancient Thebes had two.

26-7. **or the river-shrine...the ashes**: see Knox.

29-30. **our ship...**: the metaphor of the ship of state occurs frequently in the literature of the nautically minded Athenians.

34. **the plague**: some conjecture that Sophocles visualises the plague which occurred at Athens early in the Peloponnesian War. It broke out in the spring of 430, lasted for two years, and recurred in the winter of 426 for another full year. It should be noted that the plague did not include blight on plants, cattle and pregnant women, though it did claim many casualties, cf. Thucydides 2.47ff. and 3.87.

the fiery god of fever: probably Ares, the War-God, rather than Apollo. See 219.

37. **Black Death luxuriates**: literally, 'black Hades grows rich'. Hades, the god of death and the underworld, was also called Pluto. As *ploutos* is the Greek word for 'wealth' (cf. English plutocrat) and 'luxuriates' here translates *ploutizetai*, the poet is making a grim pun of a type common in tragedy.

39-40. these lines add to the favourable impression of Oedipus. The priest knows he will not be offended at being ranked lower than the gods.

44-5. **the Sphinx...the bloody tribute**: those who attempted to answer the Sphinx's riddle and failed forfeited their lives. She is said to have delivered her riddle in hexameter verses, the metre of Homer, which was also used by the Delphic oracle. The riddle was:

It is two-footed on the earth and four-footed, having one voice,
And is three-footed. Alone of all creatures that move
O'er earth and sky and sea, it changes form.
But when it goes with the support of most feet,
Then is the strength of its limbs feeblest.

Oedipus gave the right answer - man, who first uses four feet as a crawling infant, and uses a third foot, a staff, in old age.

Sphinxes vary in appearance throughout Greece, Egypt and the Middle East, but Sophocles' Sphinx seems to have a woman's head, a dog's body, wings and perhaps the feet of a bird of prey.

54. **what do you know?**: this foreshadows later developments in the play. Oedipus has already sent to Delphi; later he will consult Tiresias. See also Knox.

57. **Act now**: Oedipus has already acted, as we shall learn very soon.

69. **living all as one**: i.e. stripped of men living together in a community. The sentiment of 68-9 would appeal to the Athenians as citizens of a democratic city-state. Sophocles had already made Haemon express a similar thought, *Ant.* 739.

69-89. This speech confirms the good impression Oedipus has already made on the audience as a kind, responsible and caring ruler. It shows him already to have taken positive and sensible action.

72-3. sick...sick...sick: the Greek verb *noseō* used here usually refers to physical sickness or disease, and Thucydides uses the related noun form, *nosos*, of the plague at Athens; the verb can also mean 'to be sick at heart', 'sad' and this is what Oedipus means; he suffers mental agonies for his people. (There is no real evidence in the text of the play that Oedipus has developed physical symptoms of the plague.) However the audience who know the story may detect the other possible meaning, that Oedipus is sick, diseased, infected, because his body is unclean and tainted by the blood of Laius. (See also Knox on 80). This is one of the types of irony found in Greek tragedy, the verbal irony of the ambiguous phrase, the *double entendre*. Critics often refer to this simply as 'dramatic irony', but that term can be misleading as it is also applied to the irony of fate, events, situation etc. The irony of ambiguity is rare in English tragedy, though Shakespears's Lady Macbeth cryptically tells Macbeth that Duncan 'must be provided for' (Act 1, scene V), but it is common in Aeschylus' later plays and in Sophocles and Euripides. Thus in the *Agamemnon* Clytemnestra, giving orders for the reception of Agamemnon on his homecoming, says 'Forthwith let a purple-strewn path be prepared/That justice may lead him to a house he never expected to see.' This ambiguous irony depends for its effect on the audience recognising the hidden meaning and is therefore ideally suited to Greek tragedies which normally draw their material from familiar myths.

82. my wife's own brother: Creon and Jocasta were children of Menoeceus.

87. he's gone too long: Oedipus gives the first hint that he is less than perfect by showing impatience.

90. As often in tragedy the audience are warned of the approach of a new character and told who he is.

94-5. he's crowned...: a wreath worn on the head signified good news. Laurel is specially appropriate as being sacred to Apollo and so was presented to victors in the Pythian Games at Delphi.

103-4. Note Creon's tact and consideration towards Oedipus. Sophocles in this play makes Creon more cautious and circumspect that in his *Antigone*.

104-5. Once again Oedipus impresses with his open, democratic attitude.

118. put us straight on course: for sailing metaphor cf. on 29-30. Note Creon's tact: he is non-committal about Laius but complimentary about Oedipus.

122. the killers: note the plural; cf. 'thieves' 139. The word was particularly used in connection with murders committed within the family, and would be so recognised by the audience.

123ff. Note Oedipus' immediate and persistent enquiries. He has an inquisitive, enquiring mind throughout the play; cf. his continued enthusiasm at 249, his questioning of the Corinthian messenger, and his rejection of Jocasta's appeal at 1162 when he goes on to grill the Theban shepherd. He shows the eager desire for the truth which Thucydides, 1.22, recommends in the historian. Indeed our work 'history' comes from the Greek word meaning 'enquiry' which the earlier historian Herodotus applies to his own work. See also on 1257.

130. **to consult an oracle**: according to a later play of Euripides, *Phoenician Women* 36, Laius had gone to Delphi to ask if his exposed son was dead.

134. **all...but one**: this is the Theban shepherd who appears at 1215 and will also turn out to be the servant who should have killed the infant Oedipus.

139-40. A very natural story for the survivor to concoct. He would not have been very popular if he had reported that he had allowed one man to kill Laius and the other three menbers of his retinue. Cf. 828.

140. **a thief**: Oedipus uses the singular, where Creon had used the plural (see Knox's note). He thinks of a hired assassin leading a band, thereby revealing another trait in his character, his tendency to leap to hasty conclusions. In his attitude Oedipus seems already to be approaching the suspicions he displays in 432ff.

145. **your king**: here the Greek word for kingship (*tyrannis*) simply means 'absolute power' without the connotation that 'tyrant' has in English and sometimes in Greek. Cf. on 573 below.

146. Oedipus is appalled at the failure to conduct enquiries as he would have done.

147. **The singing, riddling Sphinx**: see on 44-5.

149. **what lay at our feet**: immediate problems - how to solve her riddle and free Thebes from her menace. Here Sophocles does his best to explain away an improbability in the story, the failure to conduct enquiries into the death of Laius.

150. Again the self-confident eager enquirer is revealed.

156-7. Note the irony; see on 72-3. Oedipus has unwittingly used a form of words which suggest other meanings to the audience who know the story. (The translation well brings out the ambiguity.) A literal translation would be: 'For on behalf of no distant dear ones (Oedipus merely means 'my wife's former husband', who, however, is also his father) but I myself for (or 'from'; the Greek could mean either) myself shall dispel this pollution.'

158-9. **to kill me too, with the same violent hand**: this

foreshadows events later in the play when Oedipus blinds himself.

160. Oedipus addresses the priests and other young suppliants; see on 1.

162. **the city**: the people, a further indication that Oedipus believes in open government. Cf. on 69.

163. **everything**: i.e. everything I can; I'll leave no stone unturned.

168. As the three actors leave the stage, the chorus pass into the orchestra. They consist of fifteen honoured Theban noblemen, who throughout show themselves religious, loyal to Thebes and devoted to Oedipus, whom they treat with great deference and, when need arises, with tact; they offer him good advice at times, but are aware of his faults.

168-244. *Parodos, first choral hymn.*
As they dance, the chorus sing prayers to Apollo, Athene and Artemis, and finally to Dionysus for help against the plague and against Ares, the War-God. See Knox.

168-79. *First strophe.*

169. **voice of Zeus**: see Knox.

170. **the gold vaults of Delphi**: literally 'Pytho rich in gold'. Sophocles uses the epithet applied in Homer to Mycenae and more recently by the Theban poet Pindar to Delphi itself in his *Pythian Odes*, poems in honour of the victors at the Pythian games at Delphi. The temple of Pythian Apollo was used as a depository for the safe keeping of gold and silver; Delphi was also enriched by the offerings and treasuries of grateful states. Visitors to Delphi can still see the Sacred Way which was lined by treasuries and votive offerings including the reconstruction of the Treasury of the Athenians, originally dedicated with spoils from the battle of Marathon.

Pytho was another name for Delphi because it was there that Apollo was thought to have killed the monstrous snake Pytho.

172-3. **my heart and I cry**: it is a convention of tragedy that the chorus speaks either in the plural or in the singular, as represented by their leader, the *coryphaeus*.

173. **Healer of Delos**: see Knox.

178. **golden Hope**: Elpis, Hope was not a particular Greek deity, simply the poet's personification of the concept. This is a poetic way of saying that the oracle speaks in answer to its questioners' hopes.

Golden = radiant, bright. The epithet appears five times in ths Ode; for its Delphic appropriateness see on 170. It was a favourite word of the Theban poet Pindar, and the first word of his *First Pythian Ode*.

180. **the first I call**: presumably because the formal appeal now starts, with preceding strophe taken as a semi-soliloquising song.

Athene is given pride of place by an Athenian poet and chorus at an Athenian festival, though only mentioned briefly. Her coupling with the twins Artemis and Apollo seems slightly unnatural but she was a formidable fighter and particularly hated Ares; see *Iliad* 5.825-63.

181. **sister**: strictly half-sister, both being daughters of Zeus.

182. **enthroned in glory**: Artemis *Eucleia* ('of the Fair Fame', 'glorious') was particularly worshipped in Boeotia, and may have had a statue in the middle of one of the market-places in Thebes. Another of her cults was that of Artemis *Agoraia*, Artemis 'of the market-place'.

184. **Apollo...heaven**: Apollo, like his twin sister Artemis, was an archer deity; he is regularly called 'far-shooting' in Homer, which is the literal meaning of the epithet translated by Fagles 'Archer...heaven'.

190-203. *Second strophe*.

203. **Evening**: the God in the West, Hades, God of darkness and Death. In the *Odyssey* Odysseus sails westwards to get to the land of the Dead.

203-17. *Second antistrophe.*

204. **numberless**: the fact that this word occurs in 191 above, in the same position in the line, makes its repetition emphatic here.

205. **her children**: the sons of Thebes, not necessarily the young.

206. **stripped of pity**: i.e. unpitied.

208. **unburied**: cf. Thuc. 2.50, recording many bodies left unburied in the Athenian plague.

the dead spreading death: for the contagion of the plague at Athens see Thuc. 2.51.

216-7. The appeal is probably to Athene, cf. 180; an Athenian audience would think of her vast statue of gold and ivory in the Parthenon on the acropolis above them, the Athena Parthenos, recently (438 B.C.) completed by Phidias. (It could, however, be Artemis, who as *Eileithyia* protected women in childbirth and had the regular epithet 'with arrows of gold'.)

218-30. *Third strophe*.

219. **raging**: the adjective (*maleros*) is usually applied to fire.

god of war: the attribution of the plague to Ares seems strange as there is no indication that Oedipus' Thebes was at war; one might have expected Apollo to send the plague as at the start of the *Iliad*. However Ares had always been regarded as an unpopular and generally destructive god, being addressed by Athene in *Iliad* 5.31 as 'scourge of mortals, stormer of cities'; cf. also *Iliad* 5.890. See Knox.

If *O.T.* was performed after 430 B.C., the prayer to banish Ares and plague from the land would have made a powerful impact on the

Athenian audience, as they thought of Attica, not Thebes.

221. cries in the onslaught: the Greek could refer both to battle cries and the cries of victims of the plague.

223. the Sea-queen: Amphitrite. Her chamber was the Atlantic.

225-6. the northern harbor: the Black Sea. Thrace, the area N.E. of Greece was regarded as particularly savage and uncivilised, and Ares was often associated with it.

231-44. *Third antistrophe. The chorus end with an appeal to Apollo, Artemis and Dionysus.*

231. Apollo...light: literally 'Lycean lord'. Apollo was called *Lykeios* probably because he was a god of light (cf. Latin *lux*), which suits the imagery of this choral song. Elsewhere the name was often interpreted as wolf-killer (*lykos* = wolf), or god of Lycia; see also on 236.

235-6. As well as being a huntress, Artemis was also a moon goddess and often depicted as holding a torch in both hands. The poet here combines the motifs of the huntress ranging over the mountains with that of the moonlight glancing down on them.

236. eastern ridges: literally 'Lycian mountains'. Sophocles chooses Lycia, a mountainous area of Asia Minor, as providing suitable terrain for hunting, but also to suggest a further association with her brother, Apollo Lykeios; see on 231 above.

238-9. Dionysus and his followers were often thought of as coming from the East and represented as wearing an Eastern headband, the *mitra*.

The story, as later told in Euripides' *Bacchae*, was that Dionysus (Bacchus) arrived in Thebes from the East but turned out to be the son of Zeus and Semele, a Theban princess.

241-3. Dionysus' female followers were called maenads (Mad Women) or Bacchantes. They honoured him with the ritual cry *evoe*, and carried torches of pinewood.

244. god of death: i.e. Ares; see on 219 above.

245-526. *First episode. Oedipus curses the murderer. Tiresias enters and a quarrel with Oedipus ensues.*

After the song of the chorus the formal spoken iambics of tragic dialogue resume. The second and subsequent dialogue scenes are called episodes because the actors return to the stage, unlike the chorus, who once they have taken up position in the orchestra, normally remain there throughout the play. Note how this powerful episode at first involves just Oedipus and the chorus, and how only two actors are used for the bitter confrontation between Oedipus and Tiresias; there is no other dialogue scene in the play needing only two actors.

245-6. Oedipus returning has heard the end of the chorus' prayer or guessed its contents. His opening words should not be taken as involving *hybris*, the impious pride which the Greeks saw as coming before a fall and being punished, usually by *atē* (ruin). A more literal translation would be 'You pray (i.e. to the gods); but as regards your prayer, if you listen to my words and act upon them, and do what the plague (*nosos*) requires...' The gods approved of those who supplemented prayer with action.

248. **a stranger**: Oedipus had spent his early years in Corinth.

249-51. Note once again Oedipus' zest for detective work.

251ff. The situation is full of dramatic irony as Oedipus curses himself lengthily and comprehensively.

254. **who**: literally 'what man'; Oedipus uses the singular.

254-5. **the son of Labdacus**: the inclusion of the father's name makes the announcement more formal. For the full family tree see p.425 of the Penguin.

274. **holy water**: before a sacrifice a firebrand from the altar was plunged into water, thus consecrating it. The water was then sprinkled on those present, purifying them.

296. **who shares our seed**: for the irony of ambiguity see on 72-3. Oedipus merely means that both he and Laius slept with Jocasta; the audience, knowing the myth, will see another meaning.

297-8. Oedipus means 'we would have shared Jocasta's children', but because of the double meaning of the Greek word used (*koinos* can mean 'related by blood' as well as 'common') the audience see another grim meaning, that the children of Laius and Oedipus would have been blood relatives, as indeed they were.

299. **his hope...disaster**: more irony; the Greek could mean either 'his hope of offspring' or 'his offspring'. Oedipus means that Laius died childless (he doesn't know what Jocasta tells him at 790ff.), but the audience could also take it as referring to Oedipus' own misfortunes.

300. **him**: i.e. Laius.

301. Again Oedipus' words bring out the irony of the situation. Laius *is* his father.

304-6. See Knox.

312. **loyal men of Thebes**: as opposed to those who might be under suspicion (307).

313. **our champion, Justice**: the Greeks regarded Justice (*dikē*) as a daughter of Zeus. Oedipus claims her as an ally because he believes his cause is just.

317-8. The chorus seem to be airing something approaching criticism of Apollo; cf. Oedipus' own account of his abortive consultation of the oracle in 869-70.

318-20. Oedipus qualifies his acquiescence in the chorus' remarks by striking an unusually cautious note.

321-2. Note once more Oedipus' energy and enthusiasm as a conscientious ruler; he will leave no stone unturned.

323. **sees with the eyes of Lord Apollo**: i.e. can see the truth as clearly as Apollo; Tiresias, as we soon shall discover, was blind.

326. The chorus' good advice is superfluous; Oedipus has already taken action, just as he had done earlier, 81-2. This time, however, he gives some credit to Creon. We have to presume that the decision had been taken and acted on off stage, in the palace, during the choral song of 168-244.

328. As at 87 Oedipus shows a trace of impatience.

330. **Which rumours?**: the detective in Oedipus is back again, cf. 249-51 above.

332. **the murderer**: once again Oedipus uses the singular.

338. **convict him**: i.e. expose him, as in fact Tiresias will.

The important part of Tiresias was probably taken by the second actor, the *deuteragonistēs*, who perhaps played the priest in the opening scene.

340ff. Note how Oedipus in his appeal to Tiresias addresses him with all the humility and respect which he himself had received earlier in the play. Tiresias' wisdom and knowledge were proverbial. He had already played an important part in *Antigone*, giving Creon good advice, which was followed too late.

350. **the murderers**: Oedipus uses the plural this time, as he gives Tiresias the gist of Creon's message of 106ff.

353. **message plucked from the birds**: Tiresias' normal method of divination was bird-watching, studying their flight, cries and behaviour when feeding.

the embers: not actually in the Greek, but Tiresias did practise divination by the study of burnt offerings, as we see in *Ant.* 1110ff. where the behaviour of the fire is studied. The entrails of sacrifical victims might also be inspected, cf. 26-7 and see Knox.

354. **mantic ways**: method of divination; *mantis* is the Greek for 'seer'.

356. **the dead**: i.e. the murder of Laius.

357. **We are in your hands**: Oedipus' phrase could have been used to address a god.

359-60. These words apparently apply to Tiresias. Later in the play they will apply more tragically to Oedipus.

366-8. Quite reasonably Oedipus is appalled by Tiresias' attitude; it would have seemed even more reprehensible in a small Greek city-state than it does to us today.

371-3. Oedipus renews his appeals to Tiresias on behalf of Thebes, as he, and presumably the chorus also, prostrate themselves before him.

375. **your own**: singular referring only to Oedipus.

377. **us**: Oedipus disregards the singular and continues to think in terms of the community.

378. **you**: i.e. Oedipus.

381-3. Here Oedipus as a conscientious ruler seems completely justified in condemning Tiresias' unhelpful attitude as ill becoming a loyal Theban.

384. **temper**: the Greek word (*orgē*) means both 'anger' and 'disposition'. For the ambiguity see also below.

385. **the one you live with**: For the irony of this phrase see on 72-3. Tiresias is right about Oedipus' hot temper, which he shows in this scene and towards Creon in the next scene. He had also killed Laius' retinue in anger; see 891. Oedipus will take the phrase to refer to his hot temper, but the audience will see that it could refer to Jocasta; the ambiguous phrase consists entirely of feminines. See Knox.

394. **hatch the plot**: Oedipus now directs the general suspicions he had voiced in 141-2. in a specific direction. The impulsive, intuitive Oedipus might well feel he had justification for his accusations.

396. **given eyes**: for the first time Oedipus taunts Tiresias with his blindness. From now on the ironical contrast will be stressed between Oedipus who has physical sight but mental blindness and Tiresias, physically blind but able to see the truth.

397. **Is that so!**: an angry retort.

398. **that decree**: the proclamation of 253, at which Tiresias had not actually been present, but it would hardly demand too much of his powers of second sight to know about it.

402-4. Oedipus, who is so quick witted, should have worked out from 401 that *he* is being accused of the murder. He knows of Tiresias' abilities; the chorus have told him (325) and he has endorsed their estimate (340), but Oedipus is angry, has already jumped to conclusions, and is so convinced of intrigue that he disregards Tiresias' words.

404-17. At this point the Greek text gives alternate lines to the two speakers. This is a regular feature of Greek tragedy known as *stichomythia* (line-speech) and is often used for heated or eager exchanges.

406. **Who primed you**: Oedipus implies that this time Tiresias is not the inspired spokesman of Apollo, but has been put up to it by someone; that someone will turn out to be Creon.

408. Oedipus is not pretending to be dull-witted, but giving Tiresias a chance to retract the accusation of 401.

409. Mild sarcasm. Oedipus who solved the riddle of the Sphinx *should* have understood.

410. **tempting me to talk**: or perhaps 'provoking me by your words'. Text and meaning are uncertain.

413-4. Tiresias repeats his accusation with the utmost clarity, but again Oedipus ignores it.

418. **you and your loved ones**: Tiresias adds to his accusation by a veiled reference to Jocasta; the plural is probably generalising, though it could be meant to include Oedipus' children.

419. **you cannot see**: Tiresias begins to reply in kind to Oedipus' taunts about blindness.

424-5. Before the end of the play Oedipus will have blinded himself, adding to the mental blindness he already has.

429. **Apollo is quite enough**: i.e. Apollo is quite strong enough to ruin you on his own.

432. Though Tiresias remains on stage, Oedipus breaks off the argument to soliloquise about his own status in life.

434. **in the heady rivalries of life**: in life that is full of competition; Greek life was very competitive, not only in politics within the small city-states, in athletics, and the theatre (with competitions between poets, actors and *chorēgoi*), but even among allies in battles, cf. Herodotus 8.93.

438-9. **the soul of trust...**: hissed out in bitter sarcasm.

440. **wizard**: translating *magos*, really a wise Persian priest who could interpret dreams, but here used contemptuously.

445. **the Sphinx...Fury**: see on 44-5 above.

445-50. Oedipus' complaint on behalf on Thebes, that Tiresias did not solve the riddle, is eminently reasonable; he does not, however, appreciate that Tiresias is controlled by Apollo.

451. **Oedipus the ignorant**: literally 'Oedipus who knew nothing', spoken sarcastically, The dramatic irony is that he *was* ignorant of the truth.

458. **this witch-hunt**: see Knox.

459. **The lash would teach you**: literally 'by suffering you would have discovered'. Sophocles adapts the common Greek saying pathei mathein 'to learn by suffering'. In his anger Oedipus has contemplated physical violence.

460-3. The chorus are tactful and impartial, suggesting to both men that thought, not anger (*orgē*) is needed. Tiresias' anger started at 385ff. and made him speak out contrary to his earlier intentions.

465. **the right to reply**: Tiresias claims one of the privileges of

Athenian democracy, equality of speech (*isēgoria*), cf. Herodotus 5.78.

474-5. the scourge...: i.e. of the dead Laius and his living relatives, his children, but more particularly his mother.

476-7. the double lash...curse: the curse of Laius, and of Jocasta when she learns the truth, will be like an avenging Fury, pursuing Oedipus with a whip with double lash.

477-9. Oedipus will be blind before the end of *O.T.* and will be an exile till the time of death which is related in Sophocles' later play, *O.C.*

480. haven: a nautical metaphor cf. 29-30 and 118 above.

481. Cithaeron: the vast mountain south of Thebes and north of Corinth, on which, as we shall discover later in the play, Oedipus was left to die by the Theban shepherd and rescued by the Corinthian, the messenger of 1012.

483-4. the wedding-march...harbour: more use of nautical metaphor. After success with the Sphinx Oedipus seems to have found a safe harbour in Jocasta's palace and her female reproductive system; cf. 480, also 1335-6 where the sexual connotations of 'harbour' are more explicit.

486. I.e. will show you who you really are, and how you and your children are alike the children of Jocasta.

493. Fair comment by Tiresias.

498-505 are in excited stichomythia.

498. Parents - who?: Oedipus is astonished by the Theban Tiresias' mention of his supposedly Corinthian parents. He still seems to think they are Polybus and Merope, cf. 852-3, but there was a slight doubt, see 858-70, now reawakened, and true to his nature Oedipus seizes on the chance for further enquiries. But Tiresias' elucidation is as unhelpful as Apollo's had been; cf. 867-70. Dawe comments: 'Sophocles quickly passes over this disturbing moment, having achieved a theatrical and psychological effect at a cost which none of his audience will notice; (Dawe *O.T.* p. 137).

499. Oedipus will make the ruinous discovery about his birth before the day is out. Lines like this and Euripides *Medea* 340 support Aristotle's theory about unity of time: 'Tragedy tries to confine itself to within one revolution of the sun or exceed it by only a little.'

503. A cryptic reference meaning that Oedipus' luck in solving the Sphinx's riddle kept him at Thebes, allowed him to marry Jocasta, and so ruined him.

507-26. In this speech Tiresias repeats more clearly what he has said before: the murderer is in Thebes (he has already told Oedipus he is the murderer), he is thought to be non-Theban (a new detail which fits Oedipus) but is really Theban born, he has married his own mother, produced children by her and killed his own father. Now we shall learn presently that Oedipus has been already told by Apollo that he will kill his father and marry his mother; see 873-5. Although Tiresias tells Oedipus to work it all out (524), he clearly hasn't given it any any thought at all, as his confidence is undiminished when he reappears at the beginning of the next scene. This brings up in acute form a general problem of the play; why is Oedipus, who was so quick and clever at solving the riddle of the Sphinx, so slow and stupid when it comes to finding out the truth about himself? One solution, that Oedipus does not hear this speech, is accepted by Knox and Fagles; see Knox's note on line 507.

508. **what I came here to say**: Tiresias is here inconsistent; he had not wanted to say anything: cf. 364-6.

513. **A stranger**: Oedipus believes he has come from Corinth.

515. **a native Theban**: born in Thebes, and so, if the standards of fifth century Athens are applied, a full citizen.

518. **towards a foreign soil**: Oedipus does not go into exile at the end of this play. In the later play, *O.C.*, covering events about twenty years later in the myth, Sophocles visualises Oedipus after having remained for many years at Thebes, eventually being exiled by Creon and going to Athens to die.

519. **a stick**: this could remind the audience of the three feet in the riddle of the Sphinx.

522-3. **he sowed the loins his father sowed**: like his father he slept with Jocasta. The Greek word here (*homosporos*) is the same adjective Oedipus had used in 296 for 'who shares our seed'. Oedipus might have recognised the allusion to Jocasta had he heard it or reflected on it!

526-572. *First stasimon. The chorus are in a dilemma because of Tiresias' accusations against Oedipus and their own feelings of trust, affection and loyalty for the king. 'Who can the murderer be?' they sing. 'He cannot escape, though he may be hiding in the most remote place. Tiresias' words worry me. I don't know what to think, but I know nothing against Oedipus. The gods are wise, but Tiresias is a mere mortal and fallible. I won't support the critics of Oedipus till they prove their words; he was the one who saved us in our hour of need.' See Knox's note.*

528. **the rocky gorge of Delphi**: Delphi stands nearly 2,000 feet above sea-level above the Pleistos gorge on a rocky platform on the S.W. slopes of Mount Parnassus.

535. **lightning-bolts**: the poet credits Apollo not with his normal

weapon, the bow, but with the thunder and lightning of his father, Zeus, as he carries out his father's purpose.

539. Parnassus: not just Delphi but all Parnassus was sacred to Apollo; it rises to over 8,000 feet.

547. the heart of Earth: a large white stone in Apollo's temple at Delphi was believed to mark the navel or centre of the earth.

555. the son of Polybus: Oedipus, as they think. A family feud between the royal houses of Thebes and Corith would have been an excuse for suspecting Oedipus of murdering Laius.

561ff. Note the contrast between the human Tiresias with his fallible skill and the superior wisdom of the two gods, heightened by the parallel positions in strophe (550) and antistrophe (561). See Knox again on 526ff.

569. the she-hawk: the Sphinx; see on 44-5.

571. the test: a metaphor of the touchstone used in testing gold. The chorus prefer the visible proofs Oedipus gave of his skill to the less tangible evidence in favour of Tiresias.

573-953. *Second episode. Quarrel of Oedipus and Creon and intervention of Jocasta. Jocasta reminisces to suggest to Oedipus that oraclemongers can be wrong, telling about their exposed child who did not kill Laius; that was done by robbers. Oedipus questions her about the time and place of the murder and about Laius' appearance. Oedipus tells her about his early life at Corinth, his visit to Delphi and the party of travellers he killed. Though the time, place and description of Laius all suggest he could have killed him, he still hopes Laius was killed by robbers, but sends for the survivor of Laius' party for questioning.*

573. King Oedipus: the Greek word *tyrannos* is used for 'king' in perhaps an ambivalent sense. Cf. 145 above, and note. It could be intended in its derogatory sense here, as Creon is angry. It is certainly used in this way at 963. The titles usually given to the play, *Oedipus Tyrannus, Oedipus Rex, Oedipus the King*, do not imply any criticism of Oedipus, but simply distinguish this play from the *O.C.*

581. is nothing simple: has more than one aspect to it. It affects his position both as a citizen of Thebes and as a member of his family.

582. a traitor: something particularly terrible in a small city-state.

583-5. Once again the chorus are diplomatic and try to pour oil on troubled waters.

585. anger: *orgē*, again. They know their Oedipus; see on 384 and 385.

588-9, 592-3. Note the continued tact of the chorus.

596-8. You...powers: Oedipus exaggerates; it seems crystal clear to him, because he has leapt to conclusions.

605. **empire**: the Greek word *tyrannis* again. Though Oedipus uses *tyrannis* here as = 'monarchy', his remarks about the acquisition of power are particularly applicable to the tyrants of Greek history, who were not kings of royal descent (*basileis*) but usually replaced oligarchies by a coup d'état, often with the support of the people or rich friends. Once established they maintained their position by mercenaries paid out of the wealth they accumulated. (A typical tyrant was Pisistratus, who controlled Athens in the middle of the sixth century).

607-9. Like Tiresias at 464-6 Creon claims *isēgoria* (equality of speech) and gets it; the Athenian audience would have approved.

611. Sarcasm by Oedipus who prides himself on his quick wit.

614. **Just one thing**: Oedipus here begins his cross-examination of Creon.

615. **stubbornness**: the term applied by Tiresias to Creon in the *Antigone*.

617. **kinsman**: accurately translating the Greek *suggenēs* (related by birth). Oedipus thinks he is using the term loosely for 'brother-in-law', but the audience will recognise the irony as Oedipus in fact is also Creon's nephew.

623-51. are all in stichomythia, apart from 638-40 immediately followed by Creon's answer in 641-3, so that Oedipus allows Creon the equality of speech he asked for in 607-8. The exchanges are excited as at first Oedipus tries to grill and browbeat Creon with a volley of quick questions, but after the pair of double lines Creon retaliates by taking the initiative, asking the questions and forcing Oedipus on the defensive.

624-5. **how long is it**: of course Oedipus knows the answer to his own question, cf. 147-9, but he is leading up to the eminently valid point of 634.

632-3. Cf. 146-9.

634. **the great seer**: more sarcasm.

640. **my killing Laius**: the Greek is ironically ambiguous. It could either mean 'this killing of mine' (i.e. as alleged by Tiresias; this is Oedipus' meaning) or 'my killing of Laius' (the actual facts, as the audience know).

642-9. The audience of democratic Athenians would have approved of Oedipus' accession to the request of 642-3 and of his subsequent admission that he shares power with Jocasta and Creon. This confirms the favourable impression of Oedipus' open, non-tyrannical attitude to government conveyed by the opening scene.

651-90. Creon is innocent and his speech probably sincere, though it reveals him as rather a mediocre and calculating person.

654-5. Compare the sentiments of the king in Shakespeare's *Henry the Fourth* Part 2: 'Uneasy lies the head that wears the crown.' (Act 3, scene 1). For Oedipus' sleepless nights see 77-9.

659. **sense of self-control**: the Greek word is *sophrosynē*, a cardinal Greek virtue, combining sensibleness, self-control and moderation. (Cf. the Delphic motto 'Nothing too much'.)

679. **clairvoyant**: a slightly contemptuous word in this context. Creon adopts a mocking tone to make his argument more persuasive.

684-5. Creon is portrayed as somewhat sententious.

690-2. Note once again the tact and good sense of the chorus.

692. **jump to conclusions**: the chorus put their fingers on an important shortcoming in Oedipus' character, but politely couch it in a generalising plural.

693-7. This self-portrait by Oedipus stresses his speed and decisiveness in action, qualities the Athenians admired and which, according to the Funeral Oration of Pericles in Thucydides, they themselves possessed. This prompts Knox to suggest that to some extent Oedipus is a reflection of the Athenians themselves; see Penguin pp.138-40.

703. **I must rule**: Oedipus uses the inoffensive verb *archein* (to rule) suggesting not tyranny but exercise of authority. Oedipus isn't being egotistical or autocratic but merely implying that without firm control anarchy may result. His thinking is much less tyrannical than that of Creon in *Antigone* 751-6.

704. **Hear him, Thebes, my city!**: an impassioned outburst by the patriotic Oedipus, still convinced Creon is a traitor.

706. **Please, my Lords**: the chorus are impartial and polite.

709ff. Jocasta speaks with the authority of her mature years and with her seniority as a queen long before Oedipus arrived on the scene. Her tone suggests that Creon may be a younger brother.

719. **stab me in the back**: Oedipus uses ambiguous phraseology which could mean actual physical violence combined with evil treachery.

736. **Sun**: see Knox.

741-5. The appeal of the chorus makes an impact and affects the action: Oedipus spares Creon. See also on 954.

744. **It's you**: consideration for Jocasta might have been a more creditable reason, but the chorus' lyrical appeal is made on behalf of Thebes and presumably anything to do with Creon, including his sister, is anathema to Oedipus in his anger. Dawe comments: 'Sophoclean characters are often fully aware that charges [of anger and inflexibility] may be brought against them, but they persist in their attitudes, true to their principles while those around them urge the

merits of moderation and compromise.' (Dawe *O.T.* on 674-5.)

747-8. **It's...themselves**: i.e. 'You'll make a rod for your own back, and rightly so,' foreshadowing events later in the play.

752. **him**: Oedipus. The chorus don't want their king in his anger to go on making a spectacle of himself in public.

754-5. See Knox.

760-1. Oedipus is offended by the impartiality of the chorus, feeling they should support their king.

761-4. Cf. 567-72.

770-1. Now that Creon is gone, Oedipus combines an expression of affection for Jocasta (cf. however on 744) with an angry, petulant and unjustified rebuke for the chorus, who can hear his words.

774 is unfair to Creon; the accusation came from Tiresias. However, it leads to Jocasta's remarkable questions in 775.

776-8. Not entirely true. Tiresias was indeed fetched at Creon's suggestion, but on Oedipus' orders; cf. 326-7.

780. Note the irony of the situation whereby Jocasta's revelations are going to have the very opposite effect on Oedipus from what she intends.

784ff. Modern readers may feel surprised that Jocasta seems to be telling Oedipus all this apparently for the first time, after years of marriage, but the improbability might not have been so apparent to Athenians seeing the play only once. The speech is excellent dramatically both in painting the background and in setting in train the slow process of Oedipus' discovery of the truth, his *anagnōrisis* or 'recognition' as Aristotle calls it, *Poetics* 11.

785-6. At this point Jocasta avoids impiety by differentiating between Apollo and his human servants, showing much the same attitude as the chorus at 563-7. She does, however, later degenerate into impiety at 944-9 and 1042-3, seeming to attribute the oracles to the god himself.

786-7. This agrees with what Apollo has told Oedipus about himself, i.e. that he will kill his father, as we shall learn later (875), but judging from 915, he doesn't seem to consider the possibility that the man he killed was his father.

789. **strangers**: i.e. non-Thebans, a fresh addition to the supposed details of the murder. Oedipus himself appears to be non-Theban, see 852ff.

792. **fastened his ankles**: we learn from 1133 that Laius drove a pin through the baby's ankles; by maiming the child he thought it less likely to be rescued. See also Knox. The exposure of unwanted babies was by no means unknown in ancient Greece, particularly if they were sickly, or girls. Though Oedipus knows there's something wrong

with *his* feet, this detail doesn't seem to worry him for the moment.

793. **trackless mountain**: Cithaeron, in this case: see on 481.

800-2. **Strange...forth**: the mention of the place in 790 has disturbed Oedipus.

804. For all his signs of agitation Oedipus typically embarks on immediate and persistent questions.

808. **Phocis**: the area of central Greece which includes Delphi and Mount Parnassus and extends to the east of them. Further east still is Boeotia, in which Thebes is situated.

809. **Daulia**: a town on the eastern foothills of Parnassus; cf. 539.

810. **a crossroads**: a Y fork, described by Sophocles at 790 as 'where three roads meet'. These are the roads to Thebes to the East, Delphi to the West and Daulia to the North.

814. **What haunts you so?**: Oedipus' fears are heightened because the time as well as the place was right.

817. **Had he reached his prime?**: i.e. how old was he?

817-9. **He was swarthy...**: the audience will certainly notice the resemblance between Laius, as described here, and Oedipus on stage, and those near enough will also see that the hair of Oedipus' mask fits the description.

820. **just**: at 269ff., earlier in the same day. As well as place and time Oedipus now has appearance to go on.

822. **I shudder to look at you**: Jocasta's fear is caused by Oedipus' obvious perturbation. If she is also frightened by Oedipus' resemblance to Laius, she seems to have got over it by the time of her speech at 937-49.

829-30. Oedipus soliloquises before continuing with his questions. Despite the story about 'thieves' (plural) he now knows beyond reasonable doubt that it was Laius he killed; obviously he still does not realise that Laius was his father.

832. **A servant**: the shepherd who appears at 1216.

834-40. Note Sophocles' skill in making the survivor behave in a highly predictable way. Rather than suffer disgrace, if not death, for letting one man kill Laius and his three companions and surviving himself, the shepherd invents the story of thieves. Then, in case Oedipus should recognise him, he asks to be sent to the country 'out of sight of Thebes' (838).

839. **Slave though he was**: loyal service was automatically expected from slaves, but this man's services went beyond the call of duty. The chorus give him a good character reference at 1224. He was born and reared in the place (1232) and clearly trusted. Despite his cowardice at the scene of the killing, he had a kind heart (1301) and tried at first to keep Jocasta's secret (1280).

843. **too much**: i.e. by cursing the killer.

847-51. These lines reveal another side to Oedipus, his capacity for warmth and affection. That the affection was reciprocated we shall see by Jocasta's attempts to relieve Oedipus' anxieties (937-49) and particularly at 953.

852ff. As the chorus have already referred to Oedipus as Polybus' son at 555, presumably Jocasta also knows the name of Oedipus' 'father' and perhaps that of his 'mother' as well. What follows, however, he seems to be telling her for the first time. The same criticisms of Jocasta's recent revelations may occur to a modern audience, but see on 784ff.

853. **a Dorian**: of noble birth, claiming descent from Dorus, one of the three sons of Hellen, the traditional ancestor of all Greeks. At first the Dorians lived in a small area north of Parnassus, the mountain north-east of Delphi, and presumably Merope is to be thought of as coming from this area.

854. **the prince of the realm**: literally 'the greatest man of the citizens there'.

860. **that...son**: the Greek could mean either that his father knew, or that he was foisted on an ignorant father; in Euripides' version of the myth in *Phoenissae* 28-31 Merope gets the child from herdsmen and convinces Polybus that he is theirs. Cf. Introduction to Oedipus the King section 1.

869-70. **Apollo spurned me...**: i.e. Apollo did not give a straight answer to a straight question.

873-5. Only at this stage in the play do the audience learn that Oedipus had been warned before ever coming to Thebes that he would marry his mother and kill his father. They would therefore have been less likely to be surprised earlier in the play at Oedipus' failure to make much of Tiresias' hints and accusations and at his failure, in his recent conversation with Jocasta, to realise that the man he killed was both Laius and his father.

881. **that very spot**: see on 810. The spot is only 17 miles from Delphi.

888-98. We know from Jocasta at 828 that the party numbered five; Oedipus, however, would only have seen four at most. The scene is variously explained, but the simplest explanation seems to be: the herald is 'the one in the lead' (888); Laius in the carriage is 'the man' of 886 and 'the old man' of 891; the 'driver' is a third man who is probably walking, leading the colts; a fourth servant, probably walking alongside or behind is not mentioned by Oedipus, but is included in 'them all'. Alternatively there is no need of an unmentioned servant if the herald and 'the one in the lead' are different. At any rate Oedipus did not see the fifth member of the party.

891. **in anger**: typical of Oedipus, cf. on 384. In *O.C.* 976 Creon tells Oedipus that his *orgē* has always been his ruin. This particular instance was perhaps the most ruinous of all.

896. **this right hand**: Oedipus (presumably) raises his hand at this point.

900. **this stranger**: again the irony of ambiguity. Oedipus merely means 'the old man I killed', but to the audience it could also refer to Oedipus himself, who arrived at Thebes as a stranger; 'this man' is often used in tragedy by a speaker referring to himself.

908-11. In fact Oedipus is already, as the audience realise, even more of an 'abomination' than he thinks; he is married to his mother.

910-23. From 899-909 Oedipus has been lamenting his fate, if he killed Laius. Now he laments a further misfortune, his enforced exile from Corinth and the danger of killing Polybus and marrying Merope.

914. **native ground**: Corinth, as Oedipus thinks.

918. **power**: divine power, deity. The Greek word used is not *theos* but *daimon,* which often suggests the deity that follows someone from birth, and so *daimōn* sometimes means 'fate'.

920-3. Events prove that Oedipus means what he says. He blinds himself later in the play and begs for exile.

922. **such corruption**: that of killing Polybus and marrying Merope, as he thinks.

930. **the worst**: i.e. his own edict and curse.

936. **the scales**: Oedipus imagines 'thieves' in one scale and himself in the other; if his scale comes down the weight of evidence is against him. It may also suggest symbolically that he is doomed, just as in *Iliad* 22, before the death of Hector, Zeus weighs the fates of Hector and Achilles and it is Hector's scale that goes down.

944. **Apollo was explicit**: Jocasta states categorically that not just prophets and spokesmen of Apollo, cf. 785, but the god himself can be fallible.

947. **They destroyed him first**: Jocasta is reticent about her own involvement.

949. **right or left**: birds flying right towards the East and the Sun were of good omen, those going left towards the West of bad omen.

950. **True, true**: Oedipus agrees rather perfunctorily with the criticisms of Apollo and prophets; he is more concerned with the herdsman and further enquiries.

952. This line shows Jocasta's love and affection for Oedipus.

954-97. *Second stasimon. While Oedipus and Jocasta are in the palace, the chorus sing, praising piety and condemning hybris and tyrannical behaviour. If injustice and impiety prosper, what point, they ask, is there is choral hymns in honour of the gods? They will give up worshipping the gods, if the oracles are found to be wrong. They pray it will not be so, but men are setting Apollo's oracles at naught and religion is at a low ebb.*

In keeping with its central position in the play, this choral song deals with a central issue in the play, the validity of the gods, their oracles and religious observances, such as the one they are now engaged in as they dance and sing at this festival. Despite their pious prayers the chorus admit that appearances are against Apollo and they end on a pessimistic note. This choral ode is closely related to the action; cf. on 741-5. Jocasta has just said that Apollo has got things wrong and Oedipus has given qualified approval to her thinking. Thus '*hybris* breeds the tyrant' (963), while it is a moral generality appropriate in any hymn, makes the audience think of what Jocasta and Oedipus have just said, and the contents of the second antistrophe (985-97) focus upon the apparent mistakes of Apollo revealed in the preceding episode. See also Knox's important note on this second stasimon.

954-62. First strophe. 'May I continue pure in word and deed and loyal to the immortal laws of heaven.'

954. **Destiny**: *moira* (fate), a power so strong that in the *Iliad* even Zeus is subject to it.

959. **Olympian Sky**: the pure sky inhabited by the gods, as opposed to Mount Olympus which is made the home of the gods in the *Iliad*.

961. The poet combines the ideas that the Laws will never forget, never be forgotten and never fall asleep in death. The dead on entering Hades passed the plain of Lethe, Forgetfulness, Oblivion. Only later was Lethe thought of as a river from which the dead souls drank and forgot the past.

963-71. First antistrophe. 'Hybris leads to tyranny, tyranny to doom. I prefer healthy competition in my state; my champion is god.'

963. **Pride**: *hybris* = impious pride and violent conduct.

the tyrant: though Sophocles often uses the Greek terms *tyrannos* and *tyrannis* generally for 'ruler', 'monarchical power', cf. 145 and 573, there is little doubt that here 'tyrant' is used in a derogatory sense to mean 'cruel and despotic ruler'. The tyrants of Greek history differed from *basileis* (hereditary kings of royal blood) in that they (or the founders of their tyrannical dynasties) were upstarts who came to power by unconstitutional, often violent, means. '*Hybris* breeds the tyrant' is a poet's way of saying 'When a man starts by acting with insolent, violent pride, eventually he degenerates into being an autocratic despot.' Sophocles, perhaps deliberately, leaves it uncertain how far the generalisations in this line, and indeed in the whole choral hymn, are to be taken to refer to Oedipus and Jocasta. Oedipus started off the play as a humble, approachable ruler but his behaviour to Tiresias and Creon verged on the hybristic and tyrannical and his reaction, as he describes it, when struck by Laius was excessive (a piece of *hybris* which resulted in the hereditary monarch being replaced by Oedipus, i.e. the *hybris* engendered a new upstart ruler, a *tyrannos*), and finally he subscribed, however, briefly, to Jocasta's impiety at 950. If Jocasta can be regarded as co-ruler, cf. 647, she is a *tyrannos* and, as her contempt for Apollo's oracles (944ff.) shows, hybristic. The audience will certainly apply the generalisations to Oedipus and Jocasta, but it is quite likely that the chorus also are deliberately criticising their rulers. They are doing what later Aristotle will say they should do: they are becoming involved in the action. As pious men they are appalled at the behaviour of their two rulers and they dissociate themselves from it, though in so doing they are unfair to Oedipus, particularly in 972-80, and exaggerate his shortcomings. Their attitude has in fact changed markedly since 567-71.

971. **champion**: having just suggested that they prefer democracy to tyranny, the chorus seem now to hint that god, not Oedipus, is their champion. Compare how in the early scenes they had looked to Oedipus as their saviour.

972-84. Second strophe.

976. By implication the chorus here pray for the punishment and destruction of Oedipus.

977. **pride**: the Greek word used here is *chlidē*, not *hybris*, though it is carrying much the same meaning in the context.

978. **profits**: implying the wealth that goes with monarchy or tyranny.

fairly: perhaps hinting at the unfair treatment of Creon.

980. **untouchable**: probably meant to be taken generally, but there is dramatic irony in the fact that it could refer to Oedipus' incestuous act.

982. **the flashing bolts of god**: probably referring to Apollo and the thunderbolts of Zeus.

984. **join the sacred dance**: i.e. perform ritual dances in honour of the gods, which is just what the chorus are now doing at Athens at a festival in honour of Dionysus. The chorus simply mean 'If the oracles are ignored, what is the point of religious observance?'

985-97. Second antistrophe.

986. **heart of Earth**: navel; see on 547.

987. **Abae**: a town in Phocis, north-east of Delphi and north of Thebes, with a rich temple of Apollo and an oracle.

988. Olympia: the sanctuary of Zeus in Elis, in the north-west Peloponnese, and scene of the Olympic Games, inaugurated in 776 B.C. and celebrated every fourth year by all Greek states. Here the reference is to divination by burnt offerings practised there.

990. for...wonder: i.e. as clear examples of the infallibility of oracles.

991. King of kings: Zeus is invited to prove his omnipotence by squashing this threat to gods and religion.

992-3. Literally 'May these things not escape the notice of you and your everlasting rule.'

997. the gods go down: it is tempting but unnecessary to see this line, and indeed much of the whole ode, as a comment by Sophocles on his own times, and on the influence of the sophists. But the chorus have merely reacted in this dramatic context with excessive pessimism to the apparent failure of the oracles and their ruler's consequent contempt for them.

998-1194. *Third episode. Jocasta worries about Oedipus' behaviour in the palace. A messenger arrives from Corinth to report the death of Polybus. Oedipus is summoned and learns he is not the son of Polybus and Merope but had been given to the messenger by a Theban. Oedipus, despite Jocasta's appeals, insists on sending for the witness of Laius' death. Jocasta rushes off stage.*

998-1000. Jocasta as a suppliant presents the same appearance as the extras in the prologue. Although she is on her way to the public temples (cf. 23-7), she addresses her prayers to the palace altars. Now a suppliant wants help *for* Oedipus, whereas early in the play suppliants had begged help *from* Oedipus. Jocasta's present piety and humility and Oedipus' reported fears make it clear that they are not to be thought as hybristic as the recent choral ode may have suggested. Note the juxtaposition of the last words of the chorus with Jocasta's present mission of piety.

1002. a man of sense: i.e. in his right mind.

1002-3. he won't..old: 'The old' prophecies are those given to Laius and now apparently disproved; and so the obvious meaning of 'the latest' ones is Tiresias' recent pronouncements. However 'the latest prophecies' could also be taken by the audience to refer to fresh developments, the indications that Oedipus may have killed Laius.

1007. Apollo: he is nearest because of his altar in front of the palace; she may also be flattering the god, suggesting he is a present help in trouble. At first sight her prayers seem to be answered at once (though not in a way she would wish) by the arrival of a cheerful messenger.

1011. Oedipus is likened to the pilot of the ship of state.

1012-4. See Knox's note.

1018. **crowned...family**: literally 'perfected', i.e. the marriage has been blessed with children. However this word *pantelēs* (by derivation 'all' and 'fulfilled') could also mean 'all-fulfilling', and could have grim undertones.

1026. **glad**: because of the extra power and wealth for Oedipus.

1027. **sorrow**: he means Oedipus has lost a father, but in fact other discoveries are in store.

1035. **Quickly**: Oedipus is on stage within five lines; the servant played by an extra does well!

1036. **You prophecies**: Jocasta soliloquises. Her impiety is increased by her being a suppliant near the altar of Apollo.

1043. **awful**: i.e. revered, august; spoken with sarcasm and contempt. We may condemn her impiety, but in her favour we should note her affection for Oedipus and eagerness to relieve his fears.

1046. See Knox's note.

1047. As always Oedipus prefers to hear at first hand; cf. 6-7.

1050. **murder**: Oedipus shows the same suspicious attitude as he has done to Tiresias and Creon earlier.

1054. **the Prophet's hearth**: the oracular hearth of Pytho (Delphi). At last Oedipus expresses his complete rejection of oracles; despite his 'True, true' at 950, he still wanted to send for the eyewitness of Laius' murder and had been beside himself inside the palace.

1063. **in hell**: in Hades, the underworld, the land of the dead; i.e. they are as dead as Polybus.

1074-5. Sigmund Freud saw great psychological truth in this remark about dreams. He disapproved, though, of Jocasta's advice in 1076 to disregard them; to him they were of great importance as proving that men are destined to be sexually attracted for the first time by their mothers and to feel their first violent hatred for their fathers. In other words we are all cursed from birth with an 'Oedipus complex' and Oedipus' fate moves us because it might have been our own. All this, of course, is Freud not Sophocles, though Freud's interpretation of *O.T.* as intended by the poet to be a tragedy of destiny is certainly tenable. (For a valuable analysis of *O.T.* and a partial rejection of this view see E.R. Dodds 'On misunderstanding the Oedipus Rex', *Greece and Rome* 1966, 37-49.)

1082. **a great blessing, joy to the eyes**: the irony is that Oedipus will soon be blind. Jocasta's affection for Oedipus makes her callous about Polybus.

1103. He answers his own question. Tragic messengers did not bring good news out of altruism.

1104-49. Now we have a protracted piece of stichomythia, mainly devoted to Oedipus' eager questions and the Corinthian's simple replies.

1105. **My boy**: spoken in a kindly and almost paternal manner, as the old man's knowledge and age enable him to treat Oedipus almost as a son, or at any rate a young man.

1116. **Nothing**: this could mean, slightly unkindly and snobbishly, 'a mere nobody'; but in the context clearly 'no relative'.

1129. **Your saviour**: Oedipus' words in 1128 were somewhat contemptuous and impolite. He is given a gentle rebuke by the old man which he well deserves.

1130. The line of questioning about pain does not follow too naturally from 1129, but gives the Corinthian a cue to mention feet.

1135. **your name**: Oedipus, 'swollen-foot', cf. 9.

1143-4. Now Jocasta knows the worst but preserves a shattered silence as long as possible.

1145. This sounds rather a naive question, but it illustrates how till this day Oedipus had only been vaguely interested in his predecessor.

1147. Questions typical of Oedipus, the eager enquirer.

1153. **the very shepherd**: the survivor of Laius' party, sent for at 952. The well-meaning chorus speak when Jocasta might have preferred their silence.

1160-2. Of course Oedipus will not stop now.

1164. **My suffering is enough**: she wants to spare Oedipus from the knowledge she now has. 'Suffering' translates *noseō*, see on 72-3. As well as being distressed, she feels unclean, diseased, because of the incest.

1164-7. The stubborn Oedipus turns rather nasty, telling Jocasta that whatever happens she will not be disgraced. He suspects her of being a snob, cf. 1175.

1166. Oedipus means 'even if the last three generations in my family have all been slaves.'

1167. **common**: low born.

1169. **know it all**: Oedipus now seeks wildly to discover the one thing Jocasta does not want him to discover; who, in fact, he is.

1172. **Your best**: Jocasta's best is for Oedipus to remain in ignorance. Once again he shows traces of impetuosity and hot temper.

1174. Characteristically Oedipus persists, making doubly sure the herdsman is fetched, though Jocasta should already have sent for him as the survivor of Laius' party; see 952.

1186. **woman's pride**: the sort of pride a woman has, i.e. in her ancestry and not like a man's pride in personal achievements.

1188. **Chance**: See Knox's note. Oedipus ironically supports Jocasta's advice at 1069ff. at the very moment when he is ignoring her warning not to look further.

1193. We may be reminded here of Polonius' advice in *Hamlet*: 'This above all, to thine own self be true.' Oedipus here, as throughout the play, is true to his own self; he just must go on till he finds out the truth; it is part of his nature and character to do so. He proves the truth of the saying of the early philosopher, Heraclitus: 'A man's character is his fate.'

1195-1214. *Third stasimon. In the form of a* hyporchēma, *a short and lively dance of joy. Cithaeron, sing the chorus, will soon be honoured by Oedipus as his birthplace. He will turn out to be the son of a god.*

Persuaded by Oedipus' confident speech, the volatile chorus have performed a volte face, after their disapproval of him in the second stasimon. The *hyporchēma* of mistaken joy is found at a similar dramatic point in other Sophoclean plays, e.g. *Ant.* 1239-58, when the chorus indulge in overoptimistic celebrations, after Creon has relented and given orders for the release of Antigone and the burial of Polynices - too late. See also Knox's note on this stasimon.

1195-1204. Strophe, balanced by antistrophe of 1204-14.

1202. **you lift our monarch's heart**: the Greek word here is *tyrannos* again, used in the plural. In contrast with 963 no disparagement is intended by the chorus' use of the word. Most scholars take 'tyrants' as a generalising plural for Oedipus, but irony is added if Jocasta is included by a chorus ignorant that Jocasta already knows Oedipus' parentage and is far from delighted; she has in fact gone into the palace to kill herself.

1203. **the wild cry**: to Apollo Paian, the Healer; see 173.

1205. **who bore you?**: kings and heroes of the myths claimed or were credited with one divine parent, e.g. Heracles, Perseus, Achilles. The chorus go one better and suggest Oedipus' parents are a god and a nymph. Note how quickly they have been converted from their forebodings of 1182. See also Knox on 1206.

1207. **Pan**: the shepherd's god with goats' hooves and horns wandered on the mountains and was a playmate of the Nymphs.

1209. **the god who loves the pastures**: one of Apollo's epithets was *nomios*, the pastoral one. Myths known to the *Iliad* had him serving as a shepherd to Laomedon at Troy and Admetus in Thessaly.

1210. **Hermes...ridges**: literally 'the lord of Cyllene'. Cyllene, a mountain in north-east Arcadia in the Peloponnese, was sacred to Hermes. As Pan was usually regarded as the son of Hermes, the chorus here put Oedipus on the same level as Pan himself.

1211. The frenzy is of the Bacchae, Dionysus' female devotees. They form the chorus of Euripides' late play, the *Bacchae*, in which they range frenzedly over Cithaeron.

1215-1310. *Fourth episode. Oedipus, who has remained on stage, is joined by the Theban servant who admits under duress that he gave a baby to the Corinthian and that it was the son of Laius and Jocasta. Oedipus now knows the whole truth and rushes off stage.*

1216. See on 90.

1217. all along: first as the survivor of Laius' party and later also as the possible recipient of the baby from Jocasta.

1228. You, old man: none too pleasantly spoken with authority to an underling.

come over here: more strictly 'look in the direction' so that Oedipus can see whether he is telling the truth as he continues with persistent and quickfire enquiries. The old man is frightened and avoids Oedipus' gaze.

1231. on the block: by auction.

1232. born...palace: and so more trusted. He speaks with a measure of pride.

1237. This man: Oedipus means the Corinthian, but it is ambiguous and could mean 'me, Oedipus', which would frighten the old Theban.

there: more strictly 'in these parts'.

1238. The Theban stalls. Apart from his fear of Oedipus, he may have recognised the Corinthian.

1248. See Knox.

1249. the rising of Arcturus: at the approximate date of the *O.T.* this would be about September 13th in our calendar. See also Knox.

the fall: the autumn.

1257-85. Perhaps the most magnificent piece of protracted stichomythia in Greek tragedy, broken only by a two-line speech at 1261-2. Despite the grim revelations Oedipus presses on; as he explains at 1285, despite everything he *must* hear.

1257. Why rake that up again: literally 'why do you ask this question?' The verb *historeō* (I enquire) is used here and several times in this scene' see on 123ff.

1258. my fine old friend: addressed to the Theban by the well-meaning Corinthian.

1259. the same man: Oedipus.

1260. The Theban's angry retort is due to self-interest. He doesn't want to be punished by Jocasta for not killing the baby as ordered. If Oedipus was that baby, he is evidence of the Theban's disobedience.

1266ff. At this point the hot temper of Oedipus, his *orgē*, flares up once more.

1269. Twist his arms back: so that he can be tied as preparation for torture. In Athenian courts slaves gave their evidence only under torture.

1280. No doubt the appeal is again mainly out of self-interest, but also perhaps out of consideration for Jocasta as he is her trusted retainer; he may also be thinking of Oedipus, who, however, rejects this effort to dissuade him from further enquiries, just as earlier he had rejected the pleas of Tiresias and Jocasta.

1289-99. Only four lines in the Greek. Far from shrinking back, Oedipus makes his questions even more quickfire and impatient. Each Greek line contains Oedipus' terse question and the equally brief answer.

1307. **O light**: see Knox's note.

1310. **the lives**: the plural is generalising, referring to Laius; cf. on 1202.

1311-50. *Fourth stasimon. The chorus lament the lot of man as exemplified by Oedipus. 'You, Oedipus, achieved the height of prosperity but are now the most wretched of men, found out by all-seeing time. I wish I had never seen you. Though you brought me salvation in the past, now you have plunged me into darkness.' See Knox's note.*

1311. **generations**: this word (*geneai*) and the general sentiment are reminiscent of Glaucus' simile in *Iliad* 6.146: 'As is the generation of leaves, so too is that of men.' This stresses the brevity and transience of human life.

1316. The metaphor suggests that human happiness is like a star that sets.

1320. **I count no man blest**: such melancholy notes occur throughout Greek literature, e.g. in the elegiac poet Theognis 167-8: 'No one is fortunate of man seen by the sun' and again later in Sophocles *O.C.* 1388ff., but they started with Homer, who has 'unhappy' as a standard epithet for mortals. Homer's treatment of the stories of Patroclus and Achilles in the *Iliad* shows that consciousness of the suffering of humanity and also of man's heroism which will develop eventually into the tragic dramas of the fifth century.

1320-30. First antistrophe.

1322. **O dear god**: 'O Zeus', an oath; the 'you' of 1320 is Oedipus.

1323-5. **the Sphinx...**: she killed herself after Oedipus solved her riddle.

1331-40. Second strophe.

1334. **name for the ages**: the Greek word used is *kleinos* (famous), the word Oedipus had applied to himself at 8.

1335. **harbour**: see note on 483-4 above.

1336. **son and father**: either both refer to Oedipus, as in 1343, or the Greek could mean 'for the son as for the father', i.e. 'for Oedipus as for Laius'.

1338. **furrows**: agricultural metaphors, sowing seed, ploughing furrows etc. for sexual intercourse are common in Greek; cf. 1388 below.

1340-50. Second antistrophe.

1340. **for all your power**: Oedipus has never attempted to conceal anything throughout the play; this may refer to his earlier attempts to thwart destiny by avoiding Corinth.

1343. **the son and the father tangling**: referring to the 'you' of 1341, that is, Oedipus.

1344-5. I.e. it would would have been better if you had never survived (or perhaps had never come to Thebes).

1349. I.e. I was revived by you, you saved me from the Sphinx.

1351-1684. *Exodos. A second messenger reports the suicide of Jocasta and the self-blinding of Oedipus. Oedipus enters and joins the chorus in a lament. Creon enters and orders Oedipus to be taken inside. Creon promises to look after Antigone and Ismene who are fetched. Oedipus says goodbye to them and asks for exile, but Creon says Apollo must decide Oedipus' fate. 'Call no man happy till you've seen his end,' conclude the chorus.*

1351. **always first in honour**: cf. 998; perhaps the implication is 'unlike Oedipus now'.

1356-7. Compare Lady Macbeth's 'Will all great Neptune's Ocean wash this blood,/Clean from my hand?'; the sentiment had already occurred in Aeschylus *The Libation Bearers* 72-4.

1357. **Nile**: see Knox.

1365-1421. Extended messenger speeches were a regular feature of tragedy. They could be regarded as an Homeric survival in tragedy, since the messenger uses a style and vocabulary with some features of epic narrative as opposed to tragic diction as he reports deaths and acts of violence which have happened off-stage, often inside the palace.

1370. **fury**: *orgē*, here in the sense of passion, the wild grief of 1180.

1383. **burst in**: into the courtyard outside the bedroom.

1384. **watch**: the bedroom doors are closed, see 1373. Unless the poet has been guilty of an oversight, we have to assume windows, chinks or peepholes in the doors or walls of the bedroom, large enough to let two or more people see in.

1388-9. The metaphor is of ploughed land, cf. 1338 above.

1390. **raging**: acting like a madman.

dark powers...way: note how Oedipus is shown where to find Jocasta by a supernatural power.

1391. Literally 'for none of us who were there near to him showed it to him.'

1393. **the twin doors**: the folding doors of the bedroom.

1399-1400. The text does not indicate how rough or gentle Oedipus was, but the sword he asked for at 1387 could have been for use first on Jocasta and then on himself.

1402-3. The brooches had long pins, here used as daggers.

1424. **my mother's** - : the messenger cannot repeat the word used by Oedipus of his relationship with his mother.

1429. **sickness**: *nosēma*, affliction both physical and mental; quite apart from his distress and the injuries to his eyes, Oedipus' body is regarded as unclean, polluted, diseased; see on 72-3.

1432-96. The dialogue is interrupted by a *kommos*, as Oedipus and the chorus share in a lament. See Knox here.

1432. When Oedipus enters the terrible sight referred to in 1431-2 will be visible by Oedipus' change of mask revealing the bloodstained sockets that had been eyes and blood all over his face. In keeping with the dramatic situation the metres used by Oedipus are more emotional than those of the chorus.

1444-6. The blind Oedipus does not know where he is going and cries out, just as Tiresias had prophesied he would do at 478-80.

1449. One iambic line, probably delivered in recitative by the chorus.

1453. **Oh again...**: 'again I say alas' is also the deathcry of Agamemnon from offstage in Aesch. *Agam.* 1345.

1455. **the stabbing daggers**: the word used for the 'stabbing' pain in Greek (*kentra* = 'prongs', 'goads') is the same as that used for the 'two prongs' with which Laius tried to strike Oedipus (893 above).

1458. **the lasting grief of pain**: painful memories.

1466. **superhuman power**: *daimōn*; see on 918 and 1390 above.

1467. **Apollo...**: Oedipus' answer is to the chorus' 'What power?' of 1466, but he goes on to qualify Apollo's part; the god was responsible for everything else but not for Oedipus' blindness; Apollo merely provided the reasons why Oedipus blinded himself. Oedipus is not going into questions of right or wrong, certainly not of moral right or wrong (cf. *O.C.* 270ff. where Oedipus stresses his moral innocence), but merely making a pious and sensible acknowledgement of the omnipotence of the gods; cf. the last line of Sophocles *Trachiniae* 'and there is nothing of these things that is not Zeus.' Oedipus is perhaps making a sinister pun (cf. 37), as *Apollon* can mean 'Destroyer'. This is reminiscent of Cassandra in Aesch. *Agam.*

1085-6.

1498. **better**: better for you in these circumstances.

1499. Normal iambic dialogue resumes, as Oedipus becomes calmer.

don't lecture me: Oedipus recovers something of his old spirit and authority.

1501. Ghosts in the underworld are pale reflections of people as they last were; so Oedipus, when dead, will be blind.

1504. **too huge for hanging**: suicide by hanging would have been inadaquate self-inflicted punishment.

1504-6. **Worse...eyes**: the Greek suggests that Oedipus is being calm and rational and following the practice of pleaders in the courts who introduce possible objections by their opponents to reject them in advance.

1526. **I'd never have**: i.e. *then* I'd never have.

my birth: i.e. my origins.

1532. **the oaks closing in**: fresh details.

1540. **fathers, brother, sons**: referring to Oedipus himself, as father and brother, more strictly half-brother, of his own children, and son of his own wife.

one murderous breed: combining the ideas of the shedding of Laius' blood and the incest with Jocasta.

1541. **brides, wives, mothers**: referring to Jocasta.

1547. **it's all right**: the chorus fear pollution from touching Oedipus; even by speaking to him they have been incurring Oedipus' own curse, cf. 272. Oedipus presumably feels that the wrath of Apollo is directed at himself alone, and that, in any case, he did not cause the pollution voluntarily.

1567. **my fears**: Oedipus had expected harsher treatment from Creon.

1572. Oedipus demands the terms of his own curse of 272.

1578-82. Here and throughout the scene Creon's caution and circumspection contrast with the hastiness and impulsiveness Oedipus has shown throughout the play.

1579-80. Oedipus considers Creon generous to bother to ask about a miserable creature like himself rather than letting him die or having him killed.

1582. Creon sounds self-righteous and unsympathetic here.

1583. **I beg you**: Oedipus corrects himself; he is no longer in a position to command.

1584. **her**: Oedipus prefers not to mention Jocasta by name.

1597. **for...strange**: Oedipus' 'strange' end is depicted by Sophocles in *O.C.*

1599. **the boys**: Eteocles and Polynices (who kill each other in Aesch. *Seven Against Thebes*, i.e. just before the opening of Soph. *Antigone*).

1602. **my two daughters**: Antigone and Ismene (who figure in the earlier play *Ant.* and the later *O.C.*).

1607. **to touch them**: Oedipus may fear Creon will forbid this, as polluting the children; see on 1547.

1609. **with all your noble heart**: Oedipus is perhaps coaxing Creon with flattery or, more likely, acknowledging Creon's 'noble' attitude of 1557-8.

1626. Cf. 1338.

1630-1. The audience will think not of Thebes of the heroic age but of contemporary Athens, where women led a comparatively secluded life but could appear in public at festivals such as the Panatheanaea, where they could enjoy the spectacle of the procession as depicted on the Parthenon frieze, or the Dionysia where they could watch the plays. As such festivals were religious occasions, the members of a polluted family would be unwelcome.

1641. I.e. he made his own mother Jocasta pregnant.

1648. **are...stroke**: Jocasta is dead, Oedipus is as good as dead.

1654. **noble Creon, touch my hand**: cf. 1607, and 1609 above.

1661. **begot you**: Dawe well comments:'Sophocles is still touching the same exposed nerve.'

1662-84. These final lines are in a different metre, called trochaics, more excited than the iambics of normal dialogue.

1671. The later play *O.C.*, see particularly 870-6, suggests Creon was not as good as his word. There is no mention of consulting Delphi and Creon opposed exile when Oedipus wanted it. Much later, when Oedipus found some pleasure in remaining at home, Creon did exile him.

1683-4. The general idea that you should not call anyone fortunate till you see how he has died had earlier been used in tragedy in Aesch. *Agam.* 928. According to Herodotus, Solon, the Athenian sage of the early sixth century, had already given this same piece of advice to Croesus, king of Lydia, who at the time was at the height of his prosperity and legendary wealth, but later was captured by Cyrus the Great of Persia. It was then that he realised the truth of Solon's words.